GAIL LOUW: COLLECTED PLAYS

T0314836

GAIL LOUW
COLLECTED PLAYS

BLONDE POISON

MISS DIETRICH REGRETS

SHACKLETON'S CARPENTER

TWO SISTERS

FOREWORD BY JAMES HOGAN

OBERON BOOKS
LONDON

WWW.OBERONBOOKS.COM

First published in 2015 by Oberon Books Ltd
521 Caledonian Road, London N7 9RH
Tel: +44 (0) 20 7607 3637 / Fax: +44 (0) 20 7607 3629
e-mail: info@oberonbooks.com
www.oberonbooks.com

A catalogue record for this book is available from the British
Library.

PB ISBN: 9781783198153
E ISBN: 9781783198146

Cover design by James Illman

For our next generation:

Peter and Hortance, Nicky and James

Andrew and Hannah, Michael

Contents

Foreword

One of my greatest pleasures is discovering new plays to add to the Oberon Books list. This happens in various ways: going to see new plays in readings or full performances or recommendations from others who have seen them. The veteran actress Virginia McKenna, star of many important films such as *Born Free* and *Carve Her Name with Pride*, enthusiastically drew my attention to *Blonde Poison*. The play was on tour at the time but soon arrived at the St. James's Theatre, London, performed by Elizabeth Counsell. I was bowled over when I read the play, and even more excited when I saw the play. Counsell was stunning in the role of Stella Goldschlag, who had been recruited by the Gestapo to inform on fellow Jews in hiding during the Nazi era.

Apart from the human tragedy of the Holocaust, the play itself is a tragedy which happens on stage, ending with a shocking coup de theatre. Goldschlag is expecting a journalist to arrive for an interview. As she prepares refreshments and chatters nervously to herself, we observe at close range how she tries to come to terms with her guilt and fails. Her suicide, if predictable, is still shocking both within the historical context in which it takes place, and the mundane existence of Goldschlag after serving a prison sentence. The skill by which Gail Louw builds up dramatic tension, using words and actions faultlessly from beginning to end is an object lesson in how to write a one-person play.

All the plays in this collection reveal Gail Louw's instinctive grasp of drama which is triggered by the human heart in crisis.

James Hogan
Publisher
Oberon Books

BLONDE POISON

Foreword

The aim of *Blonde Poison* is to tell a powerful story that resonates with themes of torture, betrayal, love, devotion and evil. The play is based on the true life story of a woman who was both a victim and persecutor during World War II. Stella Goldschlag was a Jew living illegally in war-torn Berlin when she was betrayed and tortured. When offered the chance of saving herself and her parents from deportation to Auschwitz, she agreed to be a 'Greifer' or catcher for the Gestapo and find and betray Jews in hiding. She was extraordinarily successful in this and has been 'credited' with finding and capturing 3000 Jews. The dimensions of Stella's character are vast and range from tortured victim to cruel killer, from loving daughter to betrayer of friends, from gentle lover to depraved promiscuity. She was given the name 'Blonde Poison' by the Gestapo who revelled in her wretchedness.

The issues that emerge from this story are relevant to areas of conflict throughout the world today. They relate to what makes a victim, the impact of torture on behaviour, morality and immorality and its boundaries, the ethics of self-preservation, the extent of anti-humanitarian activities in the face of personal danger, and the effect of extraordinary times on essentially ordinary people.

The play provides an unusual perspective on torture and betrayal in World War II but also resonates with events taking place throughout the world today. Torture is continually in the pages of our newspapers and our television screens; how it is often far from effective yet still used as instruments of punishment as well as means of obtaining information. It is not confined to third world countries but exists in the world's oldest democracies, and not used illegally but with the full connivance of legal authorities. The play explores how torture both physical and mental can provoke extreme behaviours and how the humanity of friends and family can be brushed aside and disposed of in favour of one's own survival.

These themes and issues provoked much discussion and debate amongst the audiences in the outings the play has had in performance so far, as well as amongst the participants in putting the play together. They relate to many aspects of people's lives. In particular, the question of 'what would I have done in that situation' was raised and explored. In a written comment by an audience participant early on in the play, Beverly Cohen said; 'We might be tempted to dismiss the play because of the detestable narcissism and evil at the core of its only character. But if we did so, we would forfeit the opportunity to explore very difficult and important questions. And we would skulk away from the fact that we are all inhabited, to a greater or lesser extent, by self-interest, fear and cowardice. To what extent can Stella's actions be justified by the inextricable dependence of torturer and tortured – in her relationship with her jailers? To what extent can any of us justify the sacrifice of other people's lives to save our own?'

Beverly Cohen continued to explore aspects of the character; 'The play works, as there are so many layers and possibilities, both in Stella's character and in the audience's reaction to her. Stella is also portrayed as a beautiful and vulnerable human being. Stella's collaboration with the Nazis was contemptible, but it required a sort of courage and flamboyance to carry it out. If we had been in her position, who knows what we would have done to save our family, to save ourselves. And would we not have been attracted to/fascinated by her charisma and her beauty at the same time as we would have been repulsed by her actions?'

The challenges associated with portraying a woman who is tormented with her past yet simultaneously refuses to admit the extent of its horrors and her personal role in its atrocities are immense, both for the actor and for me as the writer. What she says may be unrelated to what she feels and this mismatch needs to be portrayed coherently. It relies on a strong collaboration between the writer, director and actor.

I first came across the story of Stella Goldschlag at a lecture in the Wiener Library, London by the eminent historian, Roger Moorhouse. He had recently published his book *Berlin at War* and mentioned Stella in his discussion on the 'U-Boats' living illegally in Berlin during the war. I was intrigued and turned to my friend Annie sitting next to me. 'That's my next play,' I said. There were many avenues to go down; essays and pieces on the internet including a short film of children in the Goldschmidt Jewish Private School, with a definite panning across of the sweet looking young Stella sitting at a desk, looking innocently in front of her. The most important piece of work available was Peter Wyden's book *Stella* which was used extensively in the development of the play. The pictures in the book were also helpful. One showed a beautiful, smart woman, dressed in a Tyrolean hat and suit, together with a handsome young man (the brutal Rolf Isaaksohn, or Hans in the play). Another showed her in the 1960s, a wedding picture of her with her latest husband. It was of a trendy woman in a mini-skirt, but the hardened look on her face made me shudder.

I wrote the play very quickly, less than a week once all the reading and research had taken place, and felt great antipathy towards her throughout that time. It was only at an informal reading of the play with the actress Moira Brooker that I first felt anything other than antagonism. A sudden, fleeting though intense sense of pity was aroused as Stella spoke of her baby being torn from her arms.

In question and answer sessions we have had at our performances, audiences often talk of how they feel towards Stella. I am always surprised at how frequently they talk of pity as the overpowering feeling. The play was particularly written in such a way that I don't tell the audience how to feel. But I cannot suppress a sense that I want their foremost reaction to be one of vilification towards her. Certainly she did suffer appallingly, as did many others. But many others, real heroes, didn't take up the opportunity to save themselves or their loved ones at the expense of others.

This has been an exciting development for me as a writer. It has been an opportunity to write about the human condition in very real and extreme circumstances. It is also the first play I have approached where the protagonist is an entirely unattractive personality beset with human frailties and limitations, yet her massive emotional and intellectual contradictions are almost heroic. The scope of a lifetime's story featuring such dramatic and horrific activities contained within an hour and a half has tested me creatively. I believe that what the play does it to present a one-woman play that explores intricately and in a value-neutral way the horrors and vicissitudes of a woman's life in a way that is entirely accessible.

B AFTA Award-winning actress Virginia McKenna OBE and star of films including; *Born Free, A Town Like Alice* and the acclaimed *Carve Her Name With Pride*, in which Virginia starred as a female Special Operations Executive who went behind enemy lines in Nazi-occupied France, attended a performance of *Blonde Poison* at Jermyn Street Theatre in 2012.

Enamoured with the production, which stars Elizabeth Counsell and is directed by Tony Milner, Virginia is keen to share her passion for this fascinating piece of theatre as the show embarks on a national tour.

> For almost an hour and a half no one moved or coughed or fidgeted. I cannot recall ever having a similar experience as a member of a theatre audience. It was one actress, Elizabeth Counsell, alone on stage as Stella Goldschlag. The 'Blonde Poison'. Bringing to us the dark and true story of a German Jewess in Nazi Germany, a victim but also a cruel betrayer.

> A tough story to tell, but the combined skills of the author, Gail Louw, and the actress, brilliantly allowed us moments of understanding. I cannot think this work would find a better interpreter than Elizabeth Counsell – she was superb. But then, she did have a marvellous script.

Blonde Poison is based on the true story of Jewish woman Stella Goldschlag who betrayed as many as 3,000 fellow Jews during World War II. The play follows Stella, a truly complex character, as we piece together her journey and the role she embraced working for the Gestapo in war-torn Berlin.

During her extensive and hugely successful acting career, Virginia has a unique insight having played similar characters herself – most famously the World War II SOE agent Violette Szabo in the hit film *Carve Her Name with Pride* opposite Paul Scofield; a role which won her a BAFTA nomination:

You rarely get the opportunity to experience an evening in the theatre where every element of it could not be bettered: the writing, the directing, the performance, the atmosphere created... We sat riveted for the whole of the time. We could hardly breathe. It was spellbinding because it was true and uncompromising.

Stella is a mature woman who exudes an overwhelming air of vanity and confidence, intermittently juxtaposed with glimpses of anxiety as she awaits the imminent arrival of Paul Waterman, once a childhood acquaintance and now, decades later, a journalist keen to interview Stella about her experiences:

The tension, the uncertainty that you don't know what this new person is going to bring to the story and how it's going to change things or collapse things or destroy things... It's the suspense and the way it's directed by Tony Milner and the way Elizabeth performs it, that enhances that expectation.

Many plays have dealt with World War II but *Blonde Poison* is quite different. Indeed the story of Stella Goldschlag and her extraordinary success as an informer was hidden from the public domain for many years, but here we find a true account of the War yet from a very different perspective:

It's an experience in the theatre and an experience of an aspect of the War that is little known and I think it's important that as many people as possible go and see it, try to understand, just enter a new world for a brief space of time. It leaves you with so many things to think about and to me that's what a good play does.

I think this is very clever writing on a huge topic; Gail has written an extremely brilliant play.

Blonde Poison produced by New Vic Productions in association with Eastbourne Theatres, 8 November 2011, Devonshire Park Theatre.

Actress   Elizabeth Counsell

Director Tony Milner

Designer Kenneth Mellor

Lighting Gavin Davis

Production Manager Paul Debreczeny

The flat was fashionable in the 1970s, early 1980s. It is 1991 now and it looks slightly old-fashioned. But it is spotless, bright, and elegant, to a certain extent. There is a big mirror on the wall, gilded and expensive. There is one armchair in the centre of the stage, and the normal accoutrements you would expect to find – TV, telephone, VCR recorder, record player, records and a stack of fashion magazines. The kitchen and bedroom are off the lounge and a bathroom is off the bedroom, unseen by us. The front door to the flat is off a little passage from the lounge.

There is a little side table set out with elegant cups and saucers. There is a cake on a plate, a German strudel, or sachertorte.

The front door opens and STELLA walks in. She is in her early 70s but looks in her 60s. She is dressed smartly. She has been downstairs to collect her post. She is opening a letter and stops just inside the lounge to read it, clearly urgently as she does not bring it to the armchair to read in comfort. The letter is short but she reads it a couple of times. She is upset, even shocked, but dismisses it. She puts it down and walks to the tray to inspect it. She then goes to the mirror, pats her hair and checks her lipstick. Everything is in order.

She sits and picks up a magazine. As she flicks through it she starts to speak.

Nice. Clean. Everything in order. Good. Ja. It's alright. It's good.

Fifty year olds don't have teeth like mine. The dentist said, when? When was it? Last week, Frau Nietsch, your teeth are, marvellous. Ja, marvellous. That's what he said. I know Mutti, I listened to you, I always did. And you were right.

She bares her teeth. She looks at her body, checking and showing off her figure.

I'm careful with what I eat. Always careful. What do I eat at night? A little brödchen, some cheese, just a little. Salad, always salad. A little salami. I like salami. What can I do? Must I starve? No. A little salami is fine. It's good for you.

She emits a sigh of satisfaction.

Yah! I could be fifty. Forty on a good day. A dark day! But definitely fifty!

She reads the letter and is shocked.

Alzo, what can I do? I tried. I tried. So. Finished.

Nine o'clock. Too early to make the coffee.

What can I do? I can only try. So I tried. She doesn't want? She doesn't want! I can't do anything. Hey Mutti? What do you think? That's right, isn't it? You can only try. You can only go half way. You can't go further. Not if your road is barred. And I tried. Your little pünktchen, Vati. Your princess.

She looks at her watch.

She picks up another magazine and flicks through that.

She sits again and checks her watch.

Five past. Too early to make the coffee.

She flicks again.

Why is he coming? Why did I agree? Hmm? Tell me? Why did you agree? Why…did you…agree? Why did you say yes?

'Frau Nietsch, is that you? You won't believe who is here? It is Paul Waterman. Do you remember the name? Does it ring a bell?' Ring a bell, yes, a little bell. A little boy, a little boy of eleven, eleven, twelve, standing next to me in choir practice. A little boy who used to follow me, who didn't have the courage to talk to me, until one day in the snow, freezing in the snow, he said it, blurted it out, I love you Stella. I love you, a little broken, cracking voice.

(Older grown-up voice.) 'Would it be at all possible for me to come and visit you. I would be so…' Yes you would be so. I know you would be so. And do you still love me? I

hardly remember you. I hardly noticed you. A little boy freezing in the snow, saying, I love you, Stella. Go away I said to him. How could I remember you, why should I remember you? What was so special? You were one of so many who loved me. They were all in love with me. Everyone I met fell in love with me.

'Oh Frau Nietsch'. He has an American accent. 'Frau Nietsch, I would so love to come and see you. May I? I am writing a book, you see'. A book? What book? About what? Whose book? 'Why… Don't worry Frau Nietsch, please. It is, I am a journalist…' A journalist? He's almost seventy and he's a journalist! Nothing better to do? 'I'm writing a book and I would so love to come and speak with you'. Speak with me? About what? 'Your, experiences'. I have nothing to say. It is so long ago. I don't talk to journalists. 'But Stella, may I call you Stella?' No you may not! I am Frau Nietsch. But, of course, you may, I say. 'And you must call me Paul. It would so lovely, so special to see you again. May I come visit you. I will bring a cake. We will talk about the old times, our time at our dear Goldschmidt's school…'

She gets up and checks herself again in the mirror.

What does he want with me? I know what he wants. I know what they all want. How many times have they phoned, oh, Frau Nietsch, do you think it might be possible, just a short, your point of view, your experiences, your thoughts, your life. Oh, go away, I tell them all. Leave me in peace!

What's the time? Ten past nine. Too early to put on the coffee. What time did I say? Ten fifty. Yes, ten to eleven. I'll put it on at ten to eleven. The good cups. I have the good cups. You see Mutti? Such nice cups. Elegant. You would be proud.

You would be proud. You are proud. Aren't you, Mutti? Vati? Proud of your girl. Look what I've made of myself. I am still beautiful. At seventy, seventy-one, who cares.

Teeth like a young one. My hair. Always smart. Like you taught me. As you were Mutti. Always. Ahh, my Mutti. Your voice, your beautiful singing voice and how Vati accompanied you on the piano. I loved that, listening to you both in our living room. A good German family, beautiful music, beautiful singing, all beautiful.

I loved to sing. I still love to sing.

They all loved my voice. They said, Stella, you could be a singer. If I'd wanted to, I could have. But I chose to draw. You will be a great fashion designer, Mutti and Vati said to me. A big name. Stella Goldschlag, fashion maestro. Maestra. Fashion diva. Fashion granda. Fashion, queen. 'Yours will be a name to be recognised!' Vati said. Yah!

Now let's see, nine fifteen. OK, an hour and a half, I'll put on the coffee.

A good German family. A real German family. We had nothing to do with those primitives, those eastern ones, those scraggly, smelly, oh, they were disgusting. Their beards, those hats, those hats they wore. Big things, big black things. Look at me, I am Jewish. Jewish, Jewish. They have to yell it? They have to advertise it? You can see, just to look at them, their black hair, their black eyes, their hooks. They didn't need the hats as well. It was like, rubbing their noses in it.

She looks for her tape player. And puts on Schubert (e.g. 'Trout') while she is talking.

And their women! How they used to dress, with wigs. Wigs! Why do they need wigs? They have hair. And their children. Often couldn't even speak German just that terrible Yiddish. That semi-language, ersatz language. They lived in the country. What a nerve, what cheek not to speak the language of the country that gave them…well, in the early days anyway.

They were never like us. They could never be. What did they think? That they could be like us? We had culture.

We had Beethoven, Brahms, Mozart. All of them. What did they have. Hats, big black hats. That's what they had. Did they ever sit in Kempinskis, in Café Kranzler, drinking coffee, eating kuchen. No. They were at home having kichel and teiglach and blintzes, and, oogh, who knows what.

Yes, them with yellow stars, I can see. But us, us with our blonde…our smart…

He'll ask me, how did you feel wearing a yellow star. That's the sort of question that, Paul, that little boy, will ask. How did you feel? How did I feel? I loved it! How did I feel! How did *you* feel?

She turns off the music.

You don't know, do you, Paul, Paulie-waulie, because you'd gone. 1937.

'I am a veteran. I have a medal, the iron cross first class! I fought for our beloved fatherland. We do not have to leave this country. This is our fatherland. We are Germans. Just because of one lunatic? He will go, he'll be pushed. Our German people will not tolerate him, not for long.'

And when the chance came for me to go to England through the school, Mutti said 'Yes, she must go, she must get out.' But Vati, yes Vati, I've heard it called monkey love. 'We will not be parted. We are a family. I will not let my Stella leave me, leave us.'

And then there was Kristallnacht and we realised, and we tried, didn't we try, Vati? Mutti? The visa, the affidavit, Reich Flight Tax, Certificate of Harmlessness, everything needed to get out. And Uncle Leo, in St Louis, America. He tried, he did try. And finally we got on the list. We were 52,000[th] on the waiting list. Alright, they were only on 38,000, but it gave us hope. Eventually they'd get to 52,000. How long could it take? Two years. That's alright. I was still young, 18 in 1940. We had two years.

But you were long gone in 1940. Weren't you, Paulie-waulie? You didn't wait till 1940. Your father didn't think it a wrench to leave home, that we are patriots, that Germany is a safe haven. And your father didn't say we have no money, we have no contacts. Because your father did have money. Did have contacts. We'll save you, they said. Paul and family, we'll save you, because you are not just people, you are people who are encased with money. Money covers you, all round you, your eyelids, your heart. But Stella, you and your Mutti and your Vati. Where is your money? No? Pity. What a pity.

We sat, didn't we Mutti? We sat, in the flat, listening to Schubert. It will be OK, Mutti said. It will be OK, Vati said. Nobody will do anything to us. Not to us.

She hears a noise.

What was that? What's the time? Nine twenty-five. It's much too early. Can't be him. Oh my God! Don't let it be him!

She is very agitated. She opens the door.

Hello! Is anyone there?

She closes it and comes back. She calms down.

Nobody. Nothing. Not him.

She looks at the tray, looks at herself in the mirror. Checks her hair, her teeth.

I hate it when there is something in the teeth. Bit of spinach or a crumb. People walk around, they don't realise, bit of green, black seed. What do you say? You just look. You stare. Will it come out, will it drop out? It never drops out. It's there in the teeth, the black spot, it snuggles, it's found its place. It has no intention to leave.

Oishh, how I dreamt of leaving. It still seemed possible. Do you remember Mutti, the plans I had. We were going to have a band, there in St Louis. A jazz band. And I would be the singer and Manfred would be one of the musicians. There'd be four musicians and one singer. Me, the singer. Manfred, on guitar. And it was all jazz. I loved jazz in those days. We both did, Manfred and me. And it was going to happen!

(Singing.)

Toot Toot Tootsie goodbye.
Toot Toot Tootsie, don't cry.
That little choo-choo train
That takes me
Away from you, no words can tell how sad it makes me.
Kiss me Tootsie and then,

Me, and my shadow,

(Stops singing.)

I don't remember that one.

Your little pünktchen, hey Vati. You didn't like your little pünktchen singing jazz. It's degenerate, you used to say. You and Hitler, both. You could've had a nice little chat about it, how damaging to our youth, how lawless and uncontrolled. Compared to the lieder, Schubert's lieder, Schumann's lieder. Yes, I can see you sitting together, having a chat. Perhaps you'd pull out some of the ones you composed yourself. Have a look, mein Führer, you'd say. And he'd say, do you know, they're not at all bad.

You got so angry when I said that. How dare you say such things, you said. You will not sing jazz – yutz, you'd pronounce it. But I did, and I didn't listen to you. You with your lieder, going to little concerts for Jews, to sing your lieder. Excited, like a little boy. They didn't happen often and you had so many you'd written, so many you wanted to sing. They almost clapped, almost politely. But sniggered behind your back. You didn't know that, did you Vati. I didn't want you to know that. Mutti knew it. It made her despise you that little bit more.

You didn't despise Manfred, did you Mutti? You liked Manfred, with his blonde hair and his blue eyes. Manfred Kübler. My first husband. Oh, where's that picture I have of him.

She scuttles off to a box of pictures and roots around.

Here it is. The two of us. We were, good looking. Both blonde. Both looked, how shall I say it, not Jewish! *(Laughs.)* Just as much as me. I would never have fallen for someone who, my God, imagine me with a little, dark, hook for a nose, bushy eyebrows, black hat… oh my God, stop!

Hello Manfred. Look at you, so young. All your hair, no double chin, no fat nothing, no tyres round your middle, no marks, no, sign of age. Twenty. That's all. Never more than twenty.

My first love.

She notices the letter, hesitates then picks it up and reads it again.

Aishh!

She throws it down. Re-focuses.

He'll ask me about you. He'll say, what happened to Manfred. I'll say you were deported. He'll say, how. I'll say, how? What do you mean, how? How they all were. And he'll say, but why not you?

He'll be here soon. It's almost nine forty.

Why not me? Because I'm clever, that's why not.

We were safe, us, all of us, Mutti and me, working in the same factory. Manfred and Vati working in another. They needed us to do their work. They wouldn't touch us. But then people started saying they have slave labour coming from other countries, the Poles, the Litvaks, even closer to home. Soon they wouldn't need us to do their work. We started feeling less safe. And people we knew, people like us started getting letters. Present yourself. Present yourself? Like to the queen of England. May I present… Present yourself at Levetzowstrasse. Bring with you a suitcase, an overcoat, a this, a that. Two pairs of waterproof shoes. Two pairs? It must be alright with two pairs of waterproof shoes. Maybe it won't be so bad. What could they do that's so bad? Kill us? Kill us all? Don't be ridiculous. No, don't go. You mustn't go. Whatever happens, don't go. How can we not go? Where will we live? Where will we sleep? What will we do? Who will feed us, how will we eat?

And we continued in our factory. Mutti and me. Manfred and Vati. All with our yellow stars.

But I'm not a fool. While they all worked, I walked around that factory and I found a place to go to, to hide in, should it become necessary, one day, who knows. In the cellar, a little hidey-hole, big enough for me and my Mutti. And then they came, as I knew they would, February the 27th 1943. How I remember the date! That's incredible. I've still got such a memory. 'The place is surrounded by Gestapo,' a man whispered in my ears. I grabbed Mutti, and then the whistles, the screaming. Gestapo positioned at all the strategic places in and out the factory. Hundreds. We all had to walk down the stairs. Slowly, I said to Mutti. Hang back, let them all pass us, go slowly. And we were at the back of the crowd of Jews, walking through the factory and suddenly I saw our chance and we just, slipped away, disappeared, into the cellar. We climbed into the little space I had prepared. And we stood, holding each other, shh, not a word, not a breath. We heard the pleading, please, I must get an overcoat. I have nothing with me. I must tell my husband. He will wonder. He will worry. My children. Your husband will be there. Your children will be there. We do not separate families. They will all be waiting at Levetzowstrasse. Move! We waited, clutching each other, holding on for dear life. Slowly there was silence. Still we waited. We opened the door, peered out, nobody. But outside the Gestapo were still there. We walked out, tall.

Nobody stopped us. We were blonde you see. And Jews aren't blonde.

Vati worked the night shift, but Manfred was at his factory. I got a note he managed to smuggle out. I'll meet you at Roscherstrasse, tonight, it said. I went there, to our friends in Roscherstrasse. I waited there. I slept, curled up on a chair. Waiting.

(Sings.) Toot toot tootsie goodbye. Toot toot tootsie don't cry.

I always knew about sex. I don't remember when I was first told, I just knew. And I told others. I was the fount of all knowledge. How they circled me, swarmed around me. What happens then, Stella? How do you know, Stella? Tell me, tell me.

We had to be careful, didn't we Manfred? I couldn't take a chance. So we used that condom thing time and time and time again. They were tough, made out of, who knows. You weren't allowed to have condoms, then, in those days of the war. They were illegal. Ha! That's funny. I arrest you for using condoms.

Such a joke!

But he didn't come back, my Manfred. And I threw away the condom. I suppose I should have donated it to someone. People were desperate…

She looks at the letter.

My only one.

My philosophy in life is this; if you can you do and if you can't you don't cry.

Only once. Strange that. Four husbands. Only one child. Good strong condoms.

We became invisible, U-boats. Taucher. Submerged beneath the seas of Berlin. Coming up for breath and then disappearing once again. Gliding through the underworld. How frightened Mutti and Vati were. How scared all the time, how nervous, how worried. How free I felt! How tall I walked. How I smiled. My smile was clean, white, Aryan.

I went into those restaurants, I ate surrounded by police, Wehrmacht, Gestapo. What a pretty girl, they thought. What a smart girl, with such a smile, such teeth. A toothpaste advertisement, that's what she reminds me of.

And they were smart. They were clean. They had smiles too that spoke of health, strength, sunshine.

Oh who am I kidding? What, I didn't feel fear? Of course I did. Not then, not those moments when they smiled at me across the table, when they winked, or spoke to me, gnädiges Fraulein, or whispered as we passed in narrow corridors. When all they saw was the girl I wanted to be. But other times, when I walked home in the dark, back to a little room we all shared, hidden by a singer my mother knew, when I walked up the stairs, when I heard a creak and wondered who was following me. And the relief on Mutti and Vati's faces when I opened the door. 'Oh thank God,' they'd whisper. 'Where've you been? We've been going crazy, worrying, worrying'. Worrying, that's all they did. Morning to night. Day in, day out. And I'd go to sleep, on the cushions on the floor next to the single bed Mutti and Vati shared, and I'd dream I was in their arms, those straight, tall, handsome men in their uniforms, gliding in my white, flowing dress, dancing to the waltzes and the orchestras and the lights.

But anxiety, fear, lack of money seeped into the days and that early feeling of freedom disintegrated like the white clean toothpaste that gets muddied with your bad breath until it swirls down the plughole and ends in the sewers.

Rogoff came to our rescue. He forged papers. They weren't too bad but in those early days you had to make sure they didn't even sniff the rain, or the colour would drain away, water colours to water. They served their purpose. He got us ration books.

Rogoff. You became the star forger in Nazi Germany, the irritant in the corner of the eye, the fly buzzing round the head, my saviour and destroyer. How my life was affected by you, sodium and water. Explosive, Manic. Out of control.

We met as students. We sat together drawing in the design college. 'Come with me. I'll show you the good life,' he used to say. 'We'll go dancing, we'll eat in the best restaurants'. Oh yes? But he was young and a fool and he didn't have money to go to the best restaurants. So I smiled and I laughed. He loved me and I let him. Anyone could love me. And they did. 'You're so beautiful, Stella. You're so vivacious, so full of life, so…so'
…so not Jewish? Yes, that was the compliment I liked to hear most.

It was the Feige and Strassburger art school. I was fashionable. He was, an artist. An artist who felt superior to the world, above all the people around him. Apart from me. Me he looked up to. Me, he was desperate to adore. I earned some money in those days doing modelling for artists, students. I often did nude modelling. It was nothing. I wasn't bothered at all. And when I had to model for Rogoff, I refused to do it nude. Ha! You've got to keep their tongue hanging out, keep them panting. Mutti taught me that.

We lost touch in the tumult of the time and when I saw him again, he was a fellow U-boat, living illegally, just like me. We bumped into each other, in a busy street. Busy streets were good. You were anonymous, hidden in a busy street. Not noticeable, identifiable, when people walk around you. It was April 1943, I forget the exact date.

What are you doing, I asked him. He told me he was still forging papers. That was dangerous, reckless to tell people things like that. Typical of him. And then he told me he was living in a little room and asked if I wanted to see it. It sounds so innocent but it was bravado, pure bravado. He was being led by his snake, following thoughtlessly. And you know a man's snake has only one eye and no brain. I didn't have anything to lose so we got on the number 76 and stood facing each other in the crowded streetcar. We didn't talk much, we didn't want to be overheard and it's always best not to draw any attention to yourself.

I looked at him, that young man, also blonde, also good looking. His job was helping people, providing for them, people like me who were desperate and dependent on him. I knew if he told me where he lived it would be silly and he was being stupid. I said, something like that, something to that effect. Aren't you being stupid, maybe I said foolhardy, it sounds better than stupid, doesn't it? He blushed. He realised then what an idiot he'd been, how he has to learn who is boss. We got off at the next stop.

It's so annoying, him coming. All these thoughts. What do I need them for! I need to be thinking of this sort of thing? I need to start bringing up things, long forgotten things, trying to find…looking for…

She looks at the letter again – subtly.

 It just brings up these, who needs them? Honestly! I should have said no. Why didn't I? I'm a fool. I love you, he said. That little boy freezing in the snow.

I told him to go away. Leave me alone.

I should've said I'm ill, I can't manage. I'm busy.

Busy! That's a joke. Busy. I'm busy watching television. I'm busy going to have my lunch at the same canteen I go to every single day. I'm busy never seeing anyone. I'm busy not being able to sleep at night.

He'll ask about Hans. He'll know about Hans.

He'll be here soon. He'll ask about Hans.

What will I say? Oh, he was marvellous. What a wonderful man!

Will I say that? Oh, he was, a forger, you know, another forger. Good business in those days, don't you know. Did fantastic work. Not Rogoff's standard but, actually made a pretty good living of it. Well, they had to pay, didn't they? Everyone has to live! Even in times like that.

Will I tell him how I loved Hans in those days, how we made love? Oh, don't be ridiculous! Will I tell him of the hours and hours we spent in bed? Honestly! Will I say how we explored our bodies, touching every part, finding nerve endings we never knew existed, tingling with excitement, laughing at the wonderment of it all. Will I talk of the happiness I felt, of the joy? Will I say how we giggled and laughed in bed, struggling to be quiet. How we'd lie under the blankets, mocking all those people living in the flat, all those ten people living in that tiny flat. Frau Fischer with her false teeth, how she tried to keep them hidden but how can you with everyone living on top of each other. And that smelly Herr Doktor Friedland who developed a phobia of water. We'll be found out by the smell, if nothing else, we laughed. The Gestapo would just follow their noses. It would confirm their Jew as pig theory, that's for sure. And cousin Kathie…sweet cousin Kathie. We used to do things together. Little Kathie. She was about, ten then, I think. Anyway. Her father was so disapproving of us, of me. 'You've only known her five minutes and she has to come and live here. There aren't enough people living here and you have to bring her? Why doesn't she stay where she is? Why doesn't she stay with her own mother and father? Let them look after her.' He got his comeuppance, quicker than he thought!

We were partners, Hans and me. Partners in love, and… partners in, love.

We were a beautiful couple. We were known as the beautiful couple. Everyone said… I wonder where that picture is, the one with us wearing hats, looking so smart, so elegant. You'll want to see it, Paul… Ach, I haven't got the energy to look…

What made us so interested in love, in making love? The thought now… We had to be so quiet. How I used to bite his shoulder, or the pillow, when I…to stop from making, from crying out… Noiseless living, it was called. God, I remember how we couldn't even, how only three people at a time could walk around, and in stockinged feet. Don't pull the chain. Yugh.

What was the name of that café, the one we used to go to so often? It was in Mittelstrasse, do you remember? I can see it, it was quite big, lots of people in it, always lots of people. Near the opera. We knew them, they knew us. Café Bollenmüller, that's it! Of course. Café Bollenmüller. We went there so often, to get out, to get away, to spend his money.

I was sitting there once, on that day. I was waiting for them, for Hans and little Kathie. I saw my friend Angelika, my fat friend Angelika. I suppose I should have wondered how she could be fat at times like that. But I didn't. I just saw her and waved and she waved, gave a nervous sort of smile, and then disappeared. She was a Greifer, a catcher, one who helped the Gestapo find us U boats and of course in an instance they came and, straight to me, and, just, you know, that was it. I thought, bloody hell, I can't believe it, the bastards, the bitch, how could it… Thank God Hans and Kathie aren't here,

 'Stella Goldschlag'. No. NO! I am not her. Can't you see I am not her!

I walked out with them, one on each side, a little like being accompanied by a date, being escorted by two dashing… but they weren't dashing. They were anything but dashing.

Oh Mutti, it was you I thought of. You I cried for. You I despaired for.

Mutti. I felt you with me, you know, as they drove me to Burgstrasse. Now they'll have something to worry about, I thought. She was expecting it, she always knew it would happen. Now she can say, why didn't you, you should have, I wish you would have. She'll turn on Vati, she'll say, why didn't you, you should have, you could have, why didn't you. Why didn't you!

That first night they just left me. They even gave me some food and a blanket. It had seen better days, fewer fleas, but it was a blanket. And in the morning they took me into a little room. It's always a little room, and they started to question me. And then they took me back to my cell, and in the morning back to the room and sometimes it was the night that they had me in the room and back to the cell and back to the room. And the cell.

It wasn't about me. It was Rogoff they wanted. They wanted to know where Rogoff was and they thought I could tell them. They recognised his handiwork from my documents. Me they would've just put in the first cattle train eastwards. But Rogoff was something else, something worth making an effort for. And the effort focused on me. On my spine, one spot on my spine.

It's not that the cell was smaller in living space than the flat I lived in, person for person, meter for meter. It's that I was alone. All alone, isolation, solitary confinement. Nobody there, only me. And I couldn't move, couldn't go anywhere, couldn't go out, couldn't shout, couldn't speak, couldn't laugh, couldn't, who was this person, who was this woman in the cell, what was she? I didn't know her. Where were her clothes, her bed. She lay on the ground and it was wet and it was muddy and it was cold and, she didn't have that, that wasn't her life. She was smart, she was elegant, she had white teeth and blue eyes and her hair was curly, did I tell you that her blonde hair was curly. She always knew herself, she always knew she was a princess, a little Pünktchen, her Vati's little Pünktchen. She was no Pünktchen here. She was gross, she was cold, she was filthy, she was scared. Where were all the men who loved her, where were they, wanting to sleep with her, wanting to love her. They didn't want to love her here, they wanted to hurt her, to hurt her, pain, pain, sore, aching, my spine, my spine, will I ever walk again? Will I breathe again? Will I see light again, any light, daylight, night light, any, anywhere?

I don't know where he lives. I don't know anything about Rogoff. We were students together. We went to art college. It was Feige and Strassburger, that college, it doesn't exist anymore. We used to talk, we used to laugh, I would tell you, honestly, I would, I swear I would, anything, I would tell you anything, but I don't know where he lived, I don't know. How can I tell you if I don't know…he lived in Dortmunderstrasse, that's it, I am sure, he must have lived in Dortmunderstrasse. Lives in Dortmunderstrasse, try number 3. I bet it's 3. It's a small place, a little room. Try there, see if he's there. He may be. Honestly, I bet he is. I'll sleep and you go look. OK? I'll wait for you here, let me sleep.

They thought I was being clever. 'Too clever for your own good, too clever by half,' they said. I'm not clever, I just don't know.

After a while, I don't know how long, a while, a long while, they moved me. I was put in a jail with a whole lot of foreign women, Polish women, pregnant Polish women. 'Why are you here,' they asked me. 'Why are you here,' I asked them.

My teeth were hurting me. My beautiful teeth were aching. I must see a dentist, I said to the guard. I have to go to the dentist because my teeth are hurting me very badly. And they said yes, you will go to the dentist. I will beat you on your spine so that you fear you will never walk again but I will allow you to go to the dentist if your teeth are sore. And at the police dental station on Scharnhorstrasse, filled with people waiting to see the dentist and few, very few police to look after them, I walked out, yes, I did, I simply walked out, and I walked and then I ran and I ran until I stopped myself running because running is conspicuous, running can cause people to wonder why you are running, who you are running from. So I walked and I walked and when I walked into their little room and they turned and saw it was me, their Stella, they thought they were seeing a miracle. And how they cried when they saw my injuries, my broken skin, my broken body, my broken me.

'We'd better move, we'll go to a pension I was told about, it's safe, it's a good place, a good hiding place.' And we went and we arrived and, soon after, the Gestapo arrived too because it wasn't a good place, a safe hiding place.

And they took me back to the Bessemerstrasse prison barracks, to my pregnant Polish prisoners. And I sat, and I was questioned, interrogated, where does Rogoff live and I told them I didn't know and suddenly one night, one summer's night, our prison barracks in Bessemerstrasse was one of hundreds of buildings that were flattened by bombs.

The bombing started at midnight. The flames tore through the buildings. I saw those pregnant Polish women on their knees praying. Get up, I shouted, but didn't wait and ran, back and forth, into and out of the flames, a slither of a path, then blocked by fire, crawling through the rubble and the ruins and the wreckage. The smoke was everywhere, every inch of me covered, smothered and I suddenly wasn't aware and floated away, peaceful at last, but I was being grabbed, 'come on, push, help yourself!' It was a Jewish woman I knew and she pulled and I scrambled and we ran and we were out.

Out, amongst the dead and dying and corpses starting to shrivel from the heat of the bombs. I couldn't catch my breath, but had to cough, I couldn't cough but had to breathe, struggling to cough and breathe. We stumbled, we ran, we stopped, coughing, breathing. I was scratching my skin, all over, my whole skin, scratching and coughing and breathing. I couldn't open my eyes but forced, they were so, forced them open to see where I was going, where I was stumbling, scratching, coughing, falling. My clothes were shards of torn, burnt material, the shoes were bits of leather burnt into the soles of my feet.

I had to find my parents. I knew where they were. I knew they were being kept at Grosse Hamburger Strasse, waiting for deportation. For hours I walked through the incinerated streets of Berlin, like a homing pigeon through a forest fire, with only one thought, one image in mind, my Mutti and my Vati. I had to get to them. I knew when I did, it would be over. There was no hiding there, where they were. I would be with them and their future would be mine and our future would be a one-way train trip to, whatever it was out there.

I walked in and my Mutti saw me. She screamed, in horror, in joy, in shock.

They were due to be deported then, that day, but the raids had stopped it, for a day at least. But my Mutti said, 'no, I won't leave without my girl'. And as they don't like separating families, they said 'alright, we'll wait till she's healed.' In the meantime, not wanting to waste time, they tried again to find out where Rogoff lived. Again I said I did not know.

It's five past ten.

I didn't know where Rogoff lived. You see, Paul, I really didn't know where Rogoff lived.

I only ever looked for Rogoff. They all lie about the rest. Three thousand, you'll say. Lies, lies, fairy tales and lies. They lie because I am beautiful. Envy has been like a bulldog snapping at my heels, biting my shins, growling and snarling all my life.

It's not my fault. I am guilty because I am beautiful. I am guilty because I survived.

I only did it to save my parents.

I didn't know what to do. I asked them, what do you think I should do? Mutti said, 'fake cooperation, fake it till after the next deportation train to Auschwitz. Stall the Gestapo. The train after that is for Theresienstadt'. That was a better camp than Auschwitz.

'You're just faking it,' that pimply Max Abrahams said. 'I'm going to put it in my report to them. I'm sick of us hanging round waiting for him when you haven't the faintest clue where he really is.' So they put all three of our names back on the list for Auschwitz. What was I to do? What could I do? Nothing? The Gestapo, they weren't ordinary thugs you know, oh no. They had an order, to make Berlin Judenrein, Jew-free, and by God they were going to do it. And this woman, this beautiful woman, who knows Jews, knows what it means to live as a U Boat, well, she can probably help us. If we just have patience.

You see, they knew I was a devoted daughter. And my parents were perfect hostages, waiting to be deported. But, the deportation could be stopped, or at least delayed, and if you delay long enough, who knows, there is hope. And hope was the drop of water to the dying man, the crumbs to the starving. You could grow fat on hope, if you were naïve enough.

I didn't want to rely on hope. Hope was as fragile as a rain drop. You'd grab it but what can you do with a rain drop. It might slip through your fingers and it was never enough to quench your thirst.

Yes, I knew where the Jews hung out. I knew how to find them.

And Hans, my lover, he was right there, eager. 'How can I be of service, Herr Kommissar?' Kathie's father, his uncle, was his first bit of service.

You'll ask about Dobberke? Dobberke? I hardly knew him. 'How can you say that,' you'll say, 'when he was your, boss, for a year and a half.' Was it only a year and a half? It seemed like a decade. Dobberke was a policeman. He used to work in the morals section with prostitutes before the war. Prostitutes, Jews, he didn't differentiate. It was his job. He did what he was told to do. Clear the prostitutes, clear the Jews. This area must be prostitute-rein, this area must be Judenrein. Sieg heil. Yessir!

Do you know that I am a Christian? I believe in it. I want to be a Christian. I am a Christian.

This is my home, here, now. This village, far away from Berlin, far away from… *(The letter again.)*

How can you live with yourself?

I don't see many people. I see the waiter at the restaurant, canteen, fast food place. It is a fast food place because they give it to you straightaway. I go to the same place every day. I know it. They know me though there is quite a turnaround of staff. I don't want to cook. I don't see why I should cook if I don't want to. Nobody can make me do anything I don't want to. It's a fish place. I like fish.

It'll be nice seeing him, that Paul. I bet he's quite a nice man, really. He's done well for himself. A journalist. Will I still see that young boy? What will he see? You look so well, he'll say. I would never believe you were, how old? Impossible. You're still that sweet girl I fell in love with all those years ago.

I wouldn't mind seeing Lotte again. He used to follow us, Lotte and me, in the streetcar, watch us as we chatted, as we laughed. Maybe I should go to America, to visit her. Do you think it's a good idea? You'll say no, she won't want to… Oh well. What does she know? She got out.

SS Hauptsturmführer Walter Dobberke. 'Are you prepared to do your civil duty and assist us in tracking lawbreakers?' And in return you will take our names off the list.

I was free. I could go anywhere, nobody could grab me. I had a permanent pass in and out of Grosse Hamburger Strasse, the buildings where Mutti and Vati stayed and where all those people were kept who were going to be deported, and all those prisoners stuffed into cells in the basement. But I lived in an apartment in that complex, furnished and immaculate, me and Hans, and I had a green pass that I could flash at anyone who stopped me or questioned me or tried to get away from me, that and a revolver. My own revolver. And best of all, I did not have the Jewish star!

I knew them, you see, I knew where they lived, I knew where they hung out. I knew who were friends and I knew who would visit on whose birthdays. I knew who was married to Aryans and who died and who would be attending funerals, now without the protection of the Aryan spouse. I knew where they met to play cards and I knew which cafés they liked to go to, ones with easy exits and lots of people. I knew who to look for when I went to the opera and I knew how people on the run like to hide in cinemas for a bit of peace and quiet and solitude and safety. I knew the faces and I knew what to look for. And when they saw me I knew they knew who I was and what would happen to them now.

We were the beautiful couple, Hans and me. He had a soft hat which he wore stylishly, on the side. He looked like an actor and I was a movie star with my green Tyrolean hat matched with my dark green tailored suit.

How can you live with yourself?

I only went with him, accompanied him. It was him that grabbed the people, I only looked. I watched, I observed. He was the one, they were scared of him. It was only me by association, really. And he stole, it was him that took jewels, money, watches. Not me. I didn't do that. He became rich. Look at my flat. Where are my riches? 'You don't look poor', you'll say. I am. I live on social security benefits. 'What about the insurance from your last husband?' I bet he'll know. Bloody snooping, the little snitch.

I never got compensation like those rich Jews. I was a victim of fascism too. Why did I never get anything?

The beautiful couple, the blonde ghost, blonde poison. I know what they called us, what they called me.

And I never snitched on that Bettina Cohen, that time I saw her on the boat. I could've, easily. But I didn't. I noticed the fear in her eyes when she saw me, the flash they always had, like a spark that lit my heart, making me feel alive. But I didn't say anything. I didn't pull my gun, arrest her, spoil the party. And it wasn't just because I was with that Wehrmacht soldier. Heinrich, whatever. On the Wannsee for the weekend, me a Jew with him, an Aryan. Dobberke wouldn't have minded…oh God yes he would've. I could've got round him. No, I don't think so. Rassenschande, all those damned race laws, not even he… But I could've taken her in. And I didn't.

You've been speaking to people, people I've known. I bet you spoke to that Dietrich Ackerman. Silly little Dietrich. That time I saw him standing in that queue for food. He was dressed in a Hitler Youth uniform! But I recognised him. Ha, I laughed as I tapped him on the shoulder. Hello Dietrich, I said. He stopped a moment, aware that only old friends knew that name, then turned round, controlled like a tiger. 'I'm sorry miss. I don't know you. You must be mistaking me for someone else.' Oh no, matey, I certainly am not. In front of him just happened to be a Gestapo man and he was trapped between me and him. I had him, a little fly in my web, caught with the spidery juices entangling his feet like cement. I enjoyed that moment, the second before the pounce, watching his brain twirling, somersaulting, searching for an escape route. The Gestapo man turned but all he saw in front of him was a blonde, blue-eyed Hitler Youth and he hesitated, and that moment of hesitation gave Dietrich the second he needed to shove me hard in the chest and scream off into the distance. He got away.

Why did you carry on after your parents were deported?

You see how I am accused. How I am not understood. I only did it for my parents. Yes, that's what you say, but then why did you carry on after your parents were deported?

I'm so tired. Maybe I'll just put my head down a minute, here, in the armchair. A few minutes, just to sleep a bit, not to think a bit. There's still time before he comes.

She closes her eyes, then opens them slowly.

'There is an order. Berlin is to be Judenrein'. Dobberke said. 'It cannot be disobeyed. Your parents…there are no exceptions… Order of the office of Himmler himself…only some Mischlinge, some types of half Jew…I'm sorry. It's not my fault.'

I am going with them. 'No,' Mutti said. Yes, I am going with you. I won't be separated from you. 'No,' Vati said. 'You will stay. Thank God you can stay. We are not afraid.'

But I was afraid. I went with them to the station and I was afraid. I watched them climb onto the trains and I was afraid. I waited until the trains started to move, in the early hours of the morning, so the good folk of Berlin would not know that people were being sent off in cattle trains, and I was afraid. I stood there watching nothing, and I was afraid.

It was too late by then, don't you understand. You can't just stop doing what you're doing, being what you are, once you've gone that far. That's not difficult to understand, is it? Any fool can see that, surely? You don't say, OK, that's all for now, I think I'll stop now. Auf Wiedersehen. See you after the war. Look after yourself now, won't you.

What would you have done?

I wanted to be this strong woman, this smart woman.
I wanted to walk with a revolver in my bag. I wanted
the money they gave me for every person I delivered. I
wanted those little trinkets I took. I wanted the freedom
I had. I didn't want to be deported. I didn't want those
camps, I didn't want the torture. I didn't want to starve.
Who does want those things? Can you tell me, can you
find me one person who would say, yes, let me lie in filth
rather than a comfortable bed. Let me starve, die of thirst
rather than eat three meals a day, drink when I want to.
Let me walk around frightened of every sound of every
step, like a mouse, like a rat, running away, scuttling from
every source of danger. I was the queen. I was the boss.
I was the one causing all those vermin to hide, to run, to
scuttle.

Maybe I should have a quick bath before he comes, try
to relax a bit. I'm so tense. All those things, all those
questions he'll ask.

Yes, we all had lovers, of course we did. Everybody was
doing it, all over the place. You think they weren't in that
overcrowded Grosse Hamburger Strasse? When they
slept there, those Jewish men and women and children,
all together on those floorboards. Waiting to be deported.
You think they didn't there? Of course they did. We all did.
Hans with, whoever presented herself, himself, themselves.
I hated him by then. He hated me. The only difference
was that his hatred had visible consequences, bruises, black
eyes, bloodied nose. Dobberke made us marry though.
God knows why. Order, I suppose.

It's not true what people said. Vati did play in an orchestra
in Theresienstadt. They said there are no records of
them doing anything, just the date they came, and the
date they were sent to Auschwitz. They must have been
ashamed, must have kept themselves to themselves,
quiet, anonymous. Shunned, because of me. How dare

people say that? Mutti understood. Vati understood. They knew I had to, that I was just looking for Rogoff. That I was stalling. She said, stall them, Stella, stall them so we don't go to Auschwitz. And they didn't. They went to Theresienstadt, which was a better camp than Auschwitz. Only afterwards, they were sent to…

He composed lieder, like Schubert and Schumann. They were, very gentle lieder. People liked them when he sang them. They used to clap. They thought they were good. I thought they were good. Mutti thought they were good.

Why didn't they put him in an orchestra in Theresienstadt? He was a wonderful musician. He could play anything. He would've liked to be in an orchestra, to play, to sing his lieder.

I liked jazz more than lieder. He used to call it yutz. *(Sings.)* Toot toot tootsie goodbye. Toot toot tootsie don't cry. Me and my shadow…
I forget how that one goes.

Dobberke was always drunk. He liked to have violent sex with me.

I'll make some tea. It'll be good for me. Mint tea.

Leon was a prisoner. I used to sneak him food and cigarettes. It took a while for him to respond. He was a grown-up, not a boy like Hans, sick like Hans. He was tall and slender and grown-up. He was an artist too, like me. He knew how to live, even there, in that place. I just, fell in love with him. He was, only slightly Jewish. But he was so handsome and, my God, he was good in bed.

There were fewer and fewer Jews to deliver but the trains were still going. If I stopped finding Jews I could still be one to take their place. Angst was my constant companion and the swagger became a stumble, a falter. I didn't want to do it anymore. My heart was no longer in it. I walked around, I pretended, I looked, I didn't do, didn't…

She looks at the letter.

And then I became pregnant. It was February 1945.

I wanted that baby. That baby would bind me to Leon.

'You must have an abortion,' Leon said. 'And anyway, how do I know it's mine?' Of course it's yours. How could it not be yours? The others didn't mean anything to me.

And as I grew bigger the war around grew bigger and the bombings grew and the shootings grew and the destruction grew and the fear grew.

'We've got to get you out of here,' Leon said. He got a day pass from Grosse Hamburger Strasse and he took me to his house where the concierge, Frau Drescher, was leaving for her family town, Liebenwalde, 20 miles north of Berlin. 'Take her,' he said and she did.

He said he would come for me. He said he would marry me. He did, I swear he did.

I stayed there with Frau Drescher, waiting for Leon, waiting for the Russians, waiting for the baby to come. Only Leon didn't come.

The Russians raped everything in their path. Women, children, even pregnant women. Frau Drescher was raped but I hid in a space in a wall and I was not raped. Until the baby came and it felt like rape, that pain felt like rape.

But not for long. I looked at my baby, my little baby girl. My perfect little girl and I thought of my Mutti and my Vati. We were a perfect little foursome, all together, a proper family. She was so pretty, what clothes I'll dress her in, pink, bonnets, lace, lovely. And she was so good, she slept, and when she cried I fed her and I patted her and I kissed her and I loved her. She was my baby.

And when she was four months old, they took me away in handcuffs. No, you're wrong, I told those cops, those stupid provincial cops. I am a victim of Nazism, a victim of fascism. I have been persecuted too. And although finally they believed me and let me go, they did not let my baby go.

They tore my baby from my arms. They grabbed her and I held her and they pulled me and they pushed me and they took my baby from my arms. These arms. They handed her to a nurse from the Jewish hospital.

These arms held my baby, but they took her and left me, with nothing.

She was four months old. And they took her away from her mother. Me, her mother. My baby. GIVE ME BACK MY BABY!

I should have been recognised as a victim of fascism. But what did they do, those barbarians, those Jewish barbarians when they saw me, they held me down and took out a big pair of blunt scissors and all my curls, my beautiful blonde curls were chopped, shorn, torn from my scalp. Oh Mutti, you would have cried. Papa, what have they done to you, you would have said, how could they do that to you, my little Pünktchen, my princess. But they screeched as they did it, they swore, they cursed, they screamed, they spat.

I am innocent! I am a victim of fascism. I should be given compensation.

I was turned over to the police and they interrogated me. I knew interrogation. I am innocent.

I stood trial.

'Jewess Sent All Her Friends Into The Gas Chambers', the headlines screeched. The blonde poison, they said, the blonde ghost. Where did they get those witnesses? If it was true what they said about me, how did they find witnesses? They should all have been dead, if it was true, what they said about me. 'I watched her helping the Nazis load a whole lot of people onto a truck.' Why weren't you on it? How did you know? How could you know? 'I was sitting in a café and she came, walking slowly, searching every face, looking.' So why didn't I see your face, if that was true. If I found so many, thousands they said, why did *you* escape me?

'I was holding my three-year-old son who was sick with scarlet fever. She grabbed him out of my arms and took me away. He was left in the apartment alone and he died.'

I know what it means to have a child torn from my arms. Would I do that?

Max Reschke, my erstwhile colleague, Max Herr Director, he came on the stand. 'Everyone knew she was a Gestapo agent. I talked to her father in Theresienstadt, and he was deeply saddened about his daughter's activities'. *(She is shocked.)*

No, Vati was not deeply saddened. Vati was proud.

Of course they found me guilty and they sentenced me to serve ten years of hard labour in a Soviet camp.

I was 24 when I went in.

I was 34 when I came out.

I had TB and I went straight from the prison hospital into the civilian one.

Where is my baby, I said. 'She is ten, she's not a baby and she's with a good family who are looking after her well'. But she is my baby. 'You are not a fit mother'. I only had her for four months. How can you say I am not fit? 'Stella Kübler, the betrayer of her people, is not fit to be a mother. That child will have a chance in life. What chance will she have with you as her mother?' I want my baby!

I am a devoted mother, bereft of my child, a victim not only of fascism but of Eastern Bolshevism. My sin is simply that I was beautiful. Their envy does not make me guilty. They are angry because so many died. I survived, but that does not make me guilty.

And finally, I was free to find my child. Klara Baecker, Leon's name. Ten years old. Somewhere in Berlin. Waiting for her mother.

(She knocks as if knocking on a door.)

Open the door!

'I am not allowed to open the door to strangers.'

You may open the door to me.

'Who are you?'

I am your mother.

'I have no mother.'

Yes, I am your mother, open the door. Open the door!

I looked at her, my daughter. Give me a kiss. I've been looking for you for so long.

But she didn't kiss me, she didn't come to me, as I dreamed, as I'd pictured. Instead she started yelling, screaming. 'Get out, get out. Don't touch me!'

She pushed me out the door.

Don't you understand that for ten years all I've dreamt of is touching you, holding you.

She is my daughter and she has been kidnapped. 'Get out, get out,' the foster family shouted every time I came trying to take back what was mine.

She would get to know me, and she would love me. She will love me.

I took them to court. She must come and visit me. Me and my husband, Friedheim Schellenberg, also Christian, like me. Friedheim picked her up in his car at the station and brought her to our flat. 'Why must the Nazi pick me up!' She stayed for two hours, sitting on the sofa, glaring for two hours. She was made to come back, again and again.

Sometimes she said she was ill. Sometimes she came late. Sometimes she didn't come at all.

Kiss your mother.

'You're not my mother. You're a murderess.'

'Go to your mother or I'll break your bones,' my husband said.

'I'm not afraid. You killed Jews! How many did you kill? If you want to break my bones, here I am! Make a good job of it!'

I asked the courts to change her name to Schellenberg and change her religion to mine, Christian.

'God made me Jewish and I'm going to remain Jewish,' she said to the Judge. And he listened to her.

'I am not her father,' Leon said at the paternity hearing. He was still so handsome, but he wouldn't even look at me. Look at me, you, you. I waited for you. I loved you. Why won't you even look at me?

I gave up. In 1966, I gave up. I tried and then I gave up. I didn't try again.

She lives in Israel. I don't know what she does. I don't know anything about her.

She has a son. He is ten.

When I heard from you Paul, the thoughts came back to me and I wanted to know. So I found her and I wrote and she wrote back.

She lifts the letter and reads.

'I have a dream. The rifle in my hand is pointed at you and I walk through the streets of Germany until I find you. And when I do, I point the rifle directly at your head and pull the trigger. And only then will I stop atoning for the sins of my mother. I am Klara who had better not have been born.'

How can you live with yourself.

What can I say.

The doorbell goes.

Ahh, the boy in the snow. I love you Stella. I love you.

She walks to a drawer, takes out a gun. There is another knock and she shoots herself.

Blackout.

MISS DIETRICH REGRETS

Based on an idea by Felicity Dean

Miss Dietrich Regrets produced by New Vic Productions in association with Eastbourne Theatres, 20 January 2015, St James Theatre with the following cast:

MARLENE   Elizabeth Counsell

MARIA   Moira Brooker

Director Tony Milner

Production Manager Paul Debreczeny

Stage Manager Lucy Myers

Note:

No punctuation at the end of lines indicates normal interruption between the two women.

It is August, 1983. An apartment in Paris.

The room has a large bed in the centre. There are lots of things around the bed; tables, Kleenex, bottles, paper, pens, books and a telephone that is prominently placed. There is also a hotplate next to her bed and two little pots/pans, bottles, packets. There is a video cassette recorder (VCR) with piles of videos, and a tape recorder with cassettes. There is an armchair and the rest of the room can show the impression of being full of things such as wardrobe, dresser, other tables and so on. There are lots of pictures on the walls. Two bins are sitting next to the bed. Under the bed is a Limoges pitcher she uses to urinate in and a metal casserole dish for her bowel movements. Her life is in this room. She does not ever get out of bed.

It is around 2 pm. MARLENE is sleeping in the bed. She is sleeping almost sitting up on a whole range of pillows and cushions.

The entryphone rings. MARLENE is startled awake. She picks up the telephone.

MARLENE: Hello.

> *The entryphone rings again. She puts the telephone down and picks up the entryphone*

Hello?… Who?... Speak up!…Who? I can't hear you … *(Gets shocked and changes into a quasi Spanish accent.)* … No, I'm afraid you may not come up. Miss Dietrich regrets she is not available. She has gone out for the day but you may phone later… Who may I say is calling? Billy Wilder. Yes, thank you. Goodbye.

> *Puts down the entryphone*

Ohh! Kwatsch!

> *She dials the phone again but there is no answer (She is dialling MARIA.)*

> *She takes one of the little bottles and pours out a few pills, pops them in her mouth and gulps it down with a drink of whiskey from her glass besides the bed. She picks up the phone and dials.*

Sweetheart! What time is it in California? Oh, that early. Were you sleeping? No! Dreaming of me… Ahh, you are so sweet. Did you receive my little present?… itsy bitsy,teeny weeny little … panties *(Trills with laughter)*… oh good, that is essence of Marlene Dietrich *(Laughs, indicates that it is from below)*, plus a splash of Dior, of course… Sweetheart, now, those lovely little pills you send me … Yes, … Oh good. Just cover them up like you did before. It was perfect. No-one would guess, and anyway, they are from my wonderful doctor in California. No one needs ever know that we've never even… Well, I won't tell if you don't! *(Laughs)*. Now, before you go back to sleep, tell me about that dream… Ohhh… hmmmm… lovely. You naughty man! Goodnight, sweetheart. Sleep well.

She replaces the receiver.

She tries to dial MARIA again but there is no answer.

She phones Louis Bozon.

Louis? Is that…oh, kwatsch, it's that answerphone nonsense. Why do you have an answerphone? Oh, stop talking, I've heard that you're not there. …Sweetheart, why aren't you here? I am so lonely. I'm all alone. I have nothing to do. No-one has phoned. I keep phoning Maria but she doesn't pick up. I need you. I love you. You are my best friend. Come to me, please. Please.

She replaces the receiver and pushes a tape of her cabaret into the VCR.

She sings with it for a short while then drinks some more whisky.

She remembers there was an item in the newspaper that has annoyed her. She takes out her phone book to check a number, and dials.

Hello, is that the White House? …This is Marlene Dietrich. Can you put me through to the President please. …Yes, I'll wait. …Ronnie, sweetheart, hello! …Fine, thank you. How is Nancy? …Oh good… . Ja, just the same. I'm very busy. My fans keep me busy, all those letters, autographs.

… Of course I see people, all the time. Busy, busy. But not as busy you, no! …I know. …Of course. …Yes, there is something, Ronnie. This Klaus Barbie. He was a Gestapo chief. How can you even think of shielding him? It's ridiculous. You must hand him over immediately to France. They will…what…but he is not old, he is only 69. He is a young man still, he's not old at all. Of course he must be properly punished, put in front of a judge. How can you think of… Yes…good… . Thank you, Ronnie. I knew I could speak sense to you. I'll put on one of your films now, think of you… ha ha. Don't forget to send my love to Nancy. And to you, sweetheart. Goodbye. Bye.

She replaces the receiver and is pleased with herself. She puts the paper to the side and looks through her videos.

Ronald Reagan, ja, hmmm, ach nein!

And leaves them.

She picks up the phone again and dials.

Ach mensch, that bloody answerphone... *(Irritably.)* Yes, yes… . Louis, sweetheart, where are you! I need you. Why don't you come to me. I am so lonely.

She replaces the phone again.

She tries MARIA again. Puts the phone down.

Maria!

She pops a few more pills and drinks.

She suddenly hears the front door open. She starts. She hopes it is MARIA. She hears her footsteps and knows it is her. She quickly picks up a book to read but it is upside down. She doesn't look up when MARIA comes in, focusing massively on the book.

MARIA looks at her, peers at her, no response.

She walks round the bed.

MARIA: It's obviously a good book.

No response.

MARIA: You must know it well.

MARLENE: Hm.

MARIA: To be able to read it upside down!

She maintains her dignity and closes the book.

MARLENE: Oh, you're here. I thought you weren't coming again. Ever again!

MARIA: You keep phoning.

MARLENE: Nein. Not me.

MARIA: You keep phoning.

MARLENE: I must've phoned the wrong number. You know my eyesight is not so good.

MARIA: Your eyesight is fine.

MARLENE doesn't respond.

MARIA: Are you ready now?

MARLENE: Hmm?

MARIA: Are you? To talk sense. To listen!

MARLENE: Ach! Is that why you've come! To start again with me?

She picks up her book to throw at MARIA, who ducks expertly. She picks up her Limoges vase at the side of her bed (actually the vase she uses to pee in!)

MARIA: No, no! Not that! Put that down. Don't you dare!

MARLENE shrugs and puts it down.

MARIA: I dropped everything to come to you. You know? Again!

MARLENE: And why not! So you should, no? After all, I am

MARIA: I just left Bill.

MARLENE: He is only your husband.

MARIA: It's not as though it's just round the corner. It's the goddamn Atlantic

MARLENE: I am

MARIA: I've actually come to give you one last

MARLENE: Ach, enough now.

MARIA: Chance.

MARLENE: Stop it.

MARIA: Really? Stop it? Are you sure? Because then I'm off. Bye bye.

MARLENE: Maria. Come here.

MARIA stops.

MARLENE: Let me look at you.

This is something that has happened all her life. She is uncomfortable under MARLENE's stare.

MARLENE: You look peaky.

MARIA: Is that any wonder?

MARLENE: Pale. Underfed.

MARIA: I'm fine.

MARLENE: You must take more care of yourself.

MARIA: Rubbish.

MARLENE: It's Bill's fault.

MARIA: What nonsense.

MARLENE: Come give me a kiss.

Reluctantly MARIA kisses MARLENE's cheek.

MARIA: How have you been managing?

MARLENE: I'm fine. Wonderful. Can't you see?

MARIA: Well, you

MARLENE: You see that I can manage without you.

MARIA looks round at the disgusting state of the bed and surrounds.

MARIA: I do see.

MARLENE: But the truth is, I am happy to see you, Maria! It's been so long. Months and months since you were here.

MARIA: Two weeks!

MARLENE: Nonsense. It's been at least a month.

MARIA: It's been, two weeks. Less a day. Actually.

MARLENE: I see you count the days when you are away from me.

MARIA: Because you keep saying I'm never here! People phone and say, why do you never go and see her. She says you never come! How can you do this to her?

MARLENE: Well, quite right.

MARIA: But I do come, Massy. That's the point. Why do you keep telling people I don't?

MARLENE: Ach genugh jetzt. Come, I'll make you some lovely beef tea. You're looking peaky.

MARIA: So you said.

MARLENE: You don't look after yourself. Too busy with all your children, and Bill. Why do they all need looking after. They're all grown up... .Let me give you *(She ferrets about for some pills and gives them to her.)*

MARIA: What on earth

MARLENE: Take them. They'll do you good. Wonderful, I use them all the time.

MARIA: What are they?

MARLENE: Don't worry. Here, take a few.

MARIA: A few? Let me see the bottle. *(She looks.)* Massy! These are amphetamines.

MARLENE: That's alright.

MARIA: Uppers. I don't want to become a drug addict.

MARLENE: You won't. You're so tired. They'll help you. I send them to all my friends.

MARIA: In the post?

MARLENE: Of course.

MARIA puts them away.

MARLENE: Suit yourself. You're very stubborn.

MARIA: I wonder where I learnt that from!

MARLENE: I'm not stubborn. I'm as easy as

MARIA: Easy!

MARLENE: Easy.

MARIA: Massy, do you really,

MARLENE: I've always been very easy. Nobody ever complained.

MARIA: Well they wouldn't, would they? You know why? Because I'd be there weeks before you got there. Anywhere, a hotel, you know how, miraculously everything would be just the way you liked it? Well it will, I know it will surprise you to hear this, but it was because I got there first. I'd run around with half the hotel staff telling them what had to change, what had to be painted, re-decorated, re-furnished because Miss Dietrich wouldn't accept that colour, those vases, what those flowers! My God, you can't possibly put those flowers

MARLENE: What flowers?

MARIA: Whatever it was that week, that year. And the toilet here? No! it had to be moved there and besides the bathroom is too small, it will have to be another room, but one where the window is north, or south, or covered or

MARLENE: Kwatsch!

MARIA: And this door must be taken off so she can get in and out without difficulty. And I need tables along the walls for her make-up and wigs. And we need twelve extra large bath towels for when she washes her hair.

MARLENE: How you exaggerate! Ten was always enough.

MARIA: And most importantly, you must make sure there is nothing that can get in her way when she gets up at night because she must not fall. If she falls she can end up losing her legs

MARLENE: What nonsense

MARIA: Because she has a circulatory problem and there was almost no pulse in her legs.

MARLENE: You told people that!

MARIA: Yes, I told people that.

MARLENE: That I had no pulse in my legs?

MARIA: That if you fell you could end up with gangrene and have your legs amputated! The famous Dietrich legs.

MARLENE: I can't believe you told the whole world about my legs. Wie kannst Du nur? Betrayer. Assassin!

MARIA: Not the whole world.

MARLENE: As good as.

MARIA: Everything had to be out of the way, every rug, every little table, bump in the carpet. I couldn't take any chances for you.

MARLENE: I wasn't a child.

MARIA: No. You weren't a child. You were just a drunk adult with no pulse in your legs.

MARLENE: Well I didn't fall.

MARIA: No, you didn't. Thank God you didn't fall at night. *(Aside so MARLENE doesn't hear.)* You did your falling on stage!

MARLENE: No use thanking God.

MARIA: You were a full time job.

MARLENE: Thank you God. What is that for? Is he there listening to you? Do you really think so? An old man with a beard. Oh, Maria Riva is talking. I'd better stop running the world and listen to her.

MARIA: You are still a full time job.

MARLENE: I keep telling you! Ich brauche niemanden. I am perfectly fine here by myself.

MARIA: You are not! You keep phoning and phoning and phoning.

MARLENE: The fans send me things all the time, wurstchen, wonderful packets of frankfurters and you know I like to eat them raw, so there's no cooking there. Elegant trays of delicacies, herrings, from Sweden. They send them to me, marinated. Wonderful, wonderful.

MARIA: I don't know why you had to let everyone who ever works for you go. *(Aside.)* It must be because you're so easy.

It absolutely won't do. It will not!

MARLENE: What won't?

MARIA: This! This, lying here by yourself, in your bed, alone. Never ever getting up. Never! Everything happens in that bed! Look at the state of you, of this. *(Indicates bed.)*

MARLENE: Kwatsch! How many people my age with this disability would be able to keep their independence. You should be proud of me. I could be living with you. Imagine how you would like that!

MARIA: *(Aside.)* Oh God! *(To her.)* Of course I know it's amazing that you are so independent. It's wonderful

MARLENE: I heard that! You mean, thank God she's not living with me.

MARIA: Look, I worry about you.

MARLENE: Worry, worry. What have you got to worry about?

MARIA: I can't just...what've I got to worry, everything. Fire.

MARLENE: Why would there be a fire?

MARIA: Well, that hot plate, for one.

MARLENE: I do my cooking on it. It's fine. Has there ever been a fire?

MARIA: If there were a fire, how would you get out? You can't even get into that wheelchair by yourself!

MARLENE: Stop worrying so much.

MARIA: I can't tell you...I wake up at night worrying about fires. It's

MARLENE: Look at the lines on your forehead.

MARIA: *(Looking in the mirror.)* I'm not the problem.

MARLENE: No, you're fine. You ended up quite fine. Much better than when you were a child. You were so fat as a teenager.

MARIA: For God's sake.

MARLENE: It was embarrassing. A real little fettes mädchen, that was you.

MARIA: You don't have to

MARLENE: You ate so much. If you had just stuck to my sauerkraut and sausages

MARIA: They're fattening

MARLENE: You would have been fine. But you had to become an American, eat all that American crap. Hamburgers, ice cream. Fries. Cheap chocolates.

MARIA goes to the window and takes in some deep breaths to calm herself. While her back is turned, MARLENE takes the bottle that is hidden and drinks from it, and pops some pills.

MARIA: The smell is disgusting in here.

MARLENE: It isn't.

MARIA: It is. And look at your sheets. They're

MARLENE: They're fine.

MARIA: Grey and stained.

MARLENE: Kwatsch.

MARIA: Those bins of yours. Who's emptying them now since

MARLENE: Georges comes in. He's such a sweetie.

MARIA: You got rid of… Georges? The concierge? And how much are you giving him?

MARLENE: Oh, nothing much. He does it because he's such a fan. He's happy to. What does he care! To empty two bins. It's nothing.

MARIA: Nothing? It's nothing to empty someone else's – God, that is disgusting!

MARLENE: Oh for goodness sake! A little bit of pee and kaka. What does it matter! Why is this worse than dog's mess?

55

MARIA: You should've had a proper maid, or a man, someone to look after you properly.

MARLENE: You look after me.

MARIA: I'm not here

MARLENE: My point exactly!

MARIA: enough.

MARLENE: You bath me

MARIA: But you always get out of it. You find a thousand excuses to get out of it.

MARLENE: But you are so good at doing bed baths. Why must I struggle out just to be smeared in soap? And anyway, you can see my foot has no muscle

MARIA: Is it worse? Let me see.

She looks at her feet. They have developed drop foot.

MARIA: It's just awful! Look at them

MARLENE: How can you blame me? I didn't make them like that.

MARIA: But you did! Use them or lose them, you know that!

MARLENE: You come here and abuse me!

MARIA: Massy, you've got to…

MARLENE: Shout at me, make me feel that I'm disgusting.

MARIA: I'll get the bath things.

MARLENE: Me, the woman who made millions swoon. Whom the world adored. Glamorous.

MARIA: There's nothing glamorous about being in a stained, smelly bed. I'll change the sheets.

MARLENE: Not now. You've just come. We'll do it tomorrow.

MARIA: It's always not now.

MARLENE: Morgen. Tomorrow will be good.

MARIA: I know what you're doing, you know.

MARLENE: Was?

MARIA: The mess, the stink, you not having anyone so you have to do it all yourself.

MARLENE: I can manage.

MARIA: You want to be able to say, she neglected me. Maria neglected me. I was left to rot in this

MARLENE: Alles kwatsch! What nonsense!

MARIA: It's all her fault. I, who gave her everything, got nothing back when I needed her.

MARLENE: Come let me tell you who I spoke to.

MARIA: She was never around for me.

MARLENE: Ronnie.

MARIA: Me, wonderful, generous Marlene Dietrich, and look what happened at the end, in her last days.

MARLENE: I'm not planning to die tomorrow.

MARIA: What Ronnie?

MARLENE: Reagan. He was so happy to hear my voice. He was crazy about me, you know, but first Jane and afterwards Nancy, they kept such a hold on him. Honey, he said. How are you.

MARIA: So you told him how Maria neglects you.

MARLENE: I told him I was marvellous.

MARIA: You told him about your foot drop.

MARLENE: Nothing. Just marvellous.

MARIA: You are marvellous, I suppose.

MARLENE: I was

MARIA: Don't. No false modesty, please.

MARLENE: It's not false. There's nothing false about me.

MARIA: *(Laughs.)*

MARLENE: Not anymore, anyway.

MARIA: Let me look at you. You look like a … *(Softly.)* concentration camp survivor.

MARLENE: Like what? Was hast Du gesacht?

She plumps up her pillows and as she does so, MARIA feels under them and brings out two small bottles .

MARIA: What are in these?

MARLENE: Nothing. Just a little medicine if I feel ill

MARIA opens them and smells.

MARIA: Whisky!

MARLENE: It's nothing. Stop being such a dragon.

MARIA: Your drinking is

MARLENE: I was never a drinker.

MARIA: Was, is perhaps the operative word here.

MARLENE: Don't sound so

MARIA: It's absolutely out of

MARLENE: Headmistressy. You sound exactly like Fraulein what's her name, when I was six.

MARIA: Control.

MARLENE: It's not. I know exactly what I'm doing.

MARIA: And the pills. How are you getting all these pills?

MARLENE: Wouldn't you like to know!

MARIA: Unethical medical practitioners.

MARLENE: He's a lovely man. He adores me. We speak for hours.

MARIA: I know. I see your phone bill.

MARLENE: I pay for it! I am completely self-reliant.

MARIA: You're impossible.

MARLENE: I've always been impossible. But we had, different words for it, in my day.

MARIA: Mmm. What were they?

MARLENE: Fabulous. Exciting. Delicious. Luscious.

MARIA: Bohemian.

MARLENE: European.

MARIA: Berlin.

MARLENE: Civilized.

MARIA: Civilized?

MARLENE: Agh, those were the days, Maria. Twenties Berlin. The cabaret, the dancing. My first film *Morocco*,

MARIA: It wasn't your first.

MARLENE: The tails, the hat, the cigarette. The rose, the kiss on the girl's lips. *(Mocking a silly trill, covers her face with her hand as the actress does in the film.)* ha ha ha.

Silly little thing. I bedded her, you know

MARIA: Bedded? What a word.

MARLENE: I was her first one. Woman, that is.

MARIA: You were all so busy sleeping with everyone else, I'm not surprised the Weimar Republic collapsed.

MARLENE: I think she became a lesbian because of me.

MARIA: Nobody did anything other than dance and drink and sleep with each other.

MARLENE: They were such exciting times.

MARIA: But actually Morocco wasn't your first. And it wasn't made in Berlin.

MARLENE: The Americans were so shocked by our decadence. They saw it as decadent. We saw it as, European.

MARIA: Civilized.

MARLENE: Ja. You saw it as civilized, didn't you? Didn't you, sweetheart?

MARIA: It was all I knew. I was too young and, anyway, that's all I knew. Unless you have something to compare it to, what do you know? But, having a father living with another woman but being so much part of the, scene, they'd say now, I suppose. What did I know that another man, men, women slept in the same bed as my mother. It didn't mean anything to me. What did I understand?

MARLENE: You were surrounded by some of the greatest minds of the age. Von Sternberg. Remarque. …You loved Remarque,

MARIA: Yes

MARLENE: even more than I did.

MARIA: He was my friend. I had so few as a child.

MARLENE: Oh kwatsch! You had lots of friends.

MARIA: All adults.

MARLENE: They were marvellous.

MARIA: They had to be. Look who my mother was. The bodyguards, the make up woman, the wardrobe assistant.

MARLENE: They adored you.

MARIA: Some too much.

MARLENE: Ach, Du lieber himmel. Not that again. You always bring it back to that.

MARIA: Enough, enough. Let's not, come, let me, give you a massage, or something.

MARLENE: Yes, a massage. Do my foot. It could do with a good massage.

MARLENE sits up and MARIA helps organize her cushions, then sits next to her and massages her foot.

MARLENE: That's lovely.

She drinks a lot, and pops some pills when Maria isn't looking.

MARLENE: Put on some music, sweetheart. It soothes me and helps me relax, and with the massage, mm

MARIA: What shall I put on?

MARLENE looks through some records (or tapes) and hands her one.

MARLENE: Put on, this, here.

MARIA: This? Really?

MARLENE: Ja. Put it on.

MARIA puts it on. It is just applause. MARLENE enjoys it, closing her eyes. MARIA carries on massaging. It goes on for at least 15 seconds.

MARIA: *(Shakes her head in disbelief.)*

She doesn't respond, clearly loving it all.

MARLENE: Twenty four curtain calls. How they loved me.

MARIA turns it off.

MARIA: Do you mind? It all sounds a bit, samey, really.

MARLENE: Not to me.

MARIA: I suppose you had to have been there, to appreciate it.

MARLENE: You're sounding bitchy.

MARIA: Am I?

MARLENE: It's not like you. You were brought up with manners.

MARIA: Yes, listen and obey. Do what you have to and hope no-one notices you. If there's a photographer, get out of the way. Never disturb Mutti when her room is locked. Don't question Papi and certainly don't say anything about Tami!

MARLENE: Why do you always have to bring her up?

MARIA: God!

MARLENE: Papi was marvellous to her.

MARIA: Marvellous!

MARLENE: I looked after her. Mein Gott, the fortune I spent on that woman, all those hospitals, all those, procedures I paid for. A fortune, no?

MARIA: Procedures?

MARLENE: Operations, things they did to help her.

MARIA: Abortions you mean.

MARLENE: Well, why didn't she douche like the rest of us! She was such a wreck. Poor Papi having to deal with Tami, all those years. What a burden she was on him. On me.

MARIA: Oh Massy, can you hear yourself! He was so horrible to her!

MARLENE: Maria! How dare you say that about Papi!

MARIA: Poor Tami. I think of her when I'm in bed at night.

MARLENE: Thinking of Tami. Worrying about fire. Don't you ever do anything else in bed? It seems Bill needs to become a bit more active at night.

MARIA: Just keep your disgusting thoughts to yourself, Massy.

MARLENE: What, sex is disgusting now, is it? You're obviously not a virgin, not with four sons. Shall I give you some lessons?

MARIA: Stop!

MARLENE: What?

MARIA: You can be so...

MARLENE: What?

MARIA: Disgusting.

MARLENE: Me? How ridiculous. I am not at all disgusting.

I have to pee.

She takes the Limoges pitcher that is under her bed and pees in it. This can be covered by the sheets! She takes the pan and pours it into one of the bins. She rinses her hand in a bowl of water. Throughout MARIA half watches, disgusted yet unable to keep from watching.

MARLENE: Just because I tell it as it is. I'm not scared to tell the truth, I'm not a prude. I've never been a prude.

MARIA: Maybe a bit of prudishness wouldn't go amiss.

MARLENE: It's simply nature, Maria. You've had four children. You've changed nappies.

MARIA: You can't compare...

MARLENE: Don't be so, what's that American word… prissy. Zimperlich. Better word, no?

Pause.

MARIA: Prissy is better than...you don't remember the time with Bill, do you?

MARLENE: What time!

MARIA: Didn't you ever wonder why Bill never stayed with you when he came on business to America.

MARLENE: Of course he stayed with me. I liked having him to stay.

MARIA: Until the time you came home, opened your large bag, took out a pair of your pink panties and shoved them up his nose, saying

MARLENE: Smell! It's him. The President of the United States. I remember!

Jack was wonderful!

MARLENE laughs, and after a while MARIA laughs a bemused sort of laugh.

MARLENE: Don't worry about things like that, sweetheart.

MARIA: Nothing should surprise me when it comes to you. I mean it wasn't even the first time with him. And you'd slept with his father.

MARLENE: Ahh, those wonderful days in Antibes.

MARIA: My God, you'd leave Remarque to write, the dutiful hausfrau, leaving your man for the day, after loving him and feeding him, never mind your husband in the background somewhere far away,

MARLENE: And off for fun with Joe.

MARIA: And Jack.

MARLENE: Jack was more your friend in those days.

MARIA: Oh God. I adored Jack. He took me out for tea one day when he was passing through Paris. I had three days to lose weight.

MARLENE: Hmm

MARIA: And those pimples…but he came and he was so

MARLENE: Charming. He was charming. Always charming.

MARIA: Yes, to me too.

MARLENE: You see. You say you had no friends your age. But his sister Rosemary was your friend.

MARIA: The damaged child. The two misfits. We sat in the shade watching the sea, holding hands.

I loved that, all-American family.

MARLENE: Nothing is good enough for you. Always criticising!

MARIA: Their life seemed so

MARLENE: I never saw the purpose of you going to school.

MARIA: Different. Healthy, somehow.

MARLENE: Why go to school when you could go to the studio!

MARIA: It's not just about school.

MARLENE: And besides there was the kidnap attempt.

MARIA: Scare, not attempt.

MARLENE: I was so worried, so desperate, you don't remember, you were too young. But that terrible note, covered in bits of, cut out paper, just like in the films, we want $10,000, don't call the police. And they wrote 'Lindbergh business'. Oh my God, I was beside myself with worry. I phoned Papi

MARIA: Phoning Papi! In Europe!

MARLENE: Come immediately!

MARIA: As if he'd be able to get there in less than 10 days.

MARLENE: But von Sternberg, and Maurice Chevalier

MARIA: You summoned them

MARLENE: Bring guns, I said, ready to shoot.

MARIA: Oh my Lord *(Laughs.)* I remember them arriving, or maybe just the story recounted over the years. They must have been fitted out by Paramount's prop department.

MARLENE: They had bulging jackets

MARIA: With fully loaded rifles hidden in them.

MARLENE: The FBI was summoned

MARIA: And the house was full of police, all there to protect Marlene Dietrich's little girl.

MARLENE: So, you see, anyway you couldn't go to school. And at the Studio you were surrounded by all those wonderful people, all those great brains, creative…me. You learnt from me!

MARIA: I certainly did, Massy! I learnt how the light had to be just right, so that you had a little butterfly of shadow just under your nose. I learnt that gold paint could be smeared directly onto your legs for the right effect and not to worry what it does to your skin. I learnt all about beauty, how to enhance, to exaggerate, to hide. What wigs to use, how veils entice, how corsets deceive. I learnt how to make pot au feu and sauerkraut and that it was far better to cook for your man, or woman, than what happens in bed, because that isn't what's really important. But I never knew about school, about playtime and nativity plays. I didn't know about homework and school assemblies, about basketball.

MARLENE: Agh! Why would you want to know about those things?

MARIA: It was only when I had my own children and I discovered that red sandwiches are made for Valentine's Day and green ones for St Patrick's and Columbus Day they make…

MARLENE: Ridiculous!

MARIA: And it was only when I was thirty six that I'd finally had all my childhood diseases.

MARLENE: So you complain because you didn't have Chicken Pox!

MARIA: When I watched them play, that all-American family, I wanted to be, to have...

MARLENE: I cry for you.

MARIA: I don't want you to cry for me. I wanted you to look after me! To protect me! *(Pause.)* You should have protected me!

MARLENE: Sweetheart.

MARIA: Instead you were sailing away with another lover, living in a different house, and me left with the, Rhinoceros.

I thought you'd done this to punish me.

MARLENE: Me? But I didn't do anything.

MARIA: That you wanted it to happen to me.

MARLENE: How could you think

MARIA: I'd been a good girl! Why did you want me punished?

MARLENE: I didn't want you punished.

MARIA: In so many ways I was brought up to be a victim, obedient, please those in charge of me. Accept. Never question.

MARLENE: How could we know?

MARIA: She'd done her groundwork so well. Bought me that black dress I wanted.

MARLENE: You were too young for black. She seemed such a perfect governess. So right for you.

MARIA: She came in the middle of the night.

MARLENE: I know this.

MARIA: She lifted my nightgown and lay heavily on top of me, holding, touching, pushing, grunting,

MARLENE: I know

MARIA: She got up and left me and I covered myself and I shivered.

MARLENE: Why are you telling me this again?

MARIA: I lay there shivering and cold, trembling with the cold. Mutti, I screamed. But you were not there.

MARLENE: I didn't know.

MARIA: When I was granted an audience with my mother, when they finally allowed me to see my mother, but only a few minutes, I was warned, just a few minutes because your mother isn't well. And I walked in and there you lay, wan, pale, lying on the sofa. You lifted your eyes. You fluttered your eyelids.

MARLENE: Sweetheart, I said.

MARIA: And then they ushered me out because my mother was too ill.

MARLENE: I'd had an abortion for God's sake! I had my own troubles.

MARIA: Yes, it was alright for you to have an abortion.

MARLENE: Don't start that again!

MARIA: Poor Tami was treated like a pariah because she had *allowed* herself to get pregnant. Poor Papi, that stupid Tami has got herself pregnant again. Doesn't she know how to douche.

MARLENE: Why are you so angry?

MARIA stares at her.

Just because the Rhinoceros was a lesbian doesn't mean that she wasn't capable of looking after you.

What? You think I must employ people on the basis of who they sleep with?

I didn't know she'd do something like that! You can't tell by looking at someone. They don't have 'rapist' tattooed on their forehead, you know. How could I have known?

Sweetheart, maybe you should go if you are so angry. I'm expecting Louis. I'm sure he won't be so angry with me.

MARIA: What do you expect? Just accept the way you treat people, sit back and smile, because you are Marlene Dietrich, the great movie star, the glamorous grandmother, the war heroine, the woman who made Alexander Fleming tremble. The woman whose lovers caused millions of women to swoon. Frank Sinatra, Maurice Chevalier, Jean Gabin, Erich Maria Remarque, Jimmy Stewart, Yul Brynner, Edith Piaf

MARLENE: To name a few

MARIA: Yes. To name just a few. Hemingway.

MARLENE: But we were never lovers. For some reason.

I should have married Gabin. He was the only one I would have divorced Papi for, you know. But Yul, he made my heart flutter.

MARIA: *(Irritated.)* Made your heart flutter!

MARLENE: Do you think it's too much of a cliché?

MARIA: I'm sure he made your heart flutter.

MARLENE: The only one I hated after it was over.

MARIA: You certainly told me enough about it at the time. And since.

MARLENE: Don't be angry with me, sweetheart.

MARIA: I was angry. With you, with the world, but mostly with me. *(More to herself.)* It was the only way I could deal with

MARLENE: With what, sweetheart?

MARIA: Rage!

MARLENE: How was I supposed to know? You never came to me. When I spoke to you, you always said you were fine. I'm fine! Don't worry about me. I'm fine! What was I to make of that?

MARIA: Nothing,

MARLENE: You can't blame me.

MARIA: No.

MARLENE: I won't let you blame me!

MARIA: Of course not. Of course Marlene Dietrich is not to be blamed.

MARLENE: You sound bitter and older than you should.

MARIA: 'I am fine' doesn't always mean, 'I am fine'.

MARLENE: And how am I supposed to know when I am fine means I am not fine.

MARIA: Mothers are supposed to know!

MARLENE: Yes, if you're a mother who does nothing but be a mother. Those sad creatures who have nothing in their lives but their children. Who live for their children. My child is this, my child is that. I was always much more than just a mother!

MARIA: You were always much more, but as a mother, you were

MARLENE: Don't say, less.

MARIA: Why shouldn't I?

MARLENE: It sounds so, more, less. As if you're trying to be poetic, dramatic. I was a mother, simply that.

MARIA: You were a movie star. That's what defined you.

MARLENE: Anyway, I always adored you.

MARIA: Somewhere way down the list of those you adored.

MARLENE: No. I adored you the most.

MARIA: Now, you adore me the most, now, because now there is no one else to adore.

MARLENE: There are millions. All my fan mail, all my phone calls, letters. I don't need you.

MARIA: Don't you? Really?

MARLENE: You can go. You could always go.

The entry phone suddenly rings.

MARLENE: Hello? …Who? …Speak up! …Who? I can't hear you... *(Changes into a quasi Spanish accent)* …No, I'm afraid you may come up. Miss Dietrich regrets she is not available. She has gone out for the day but you may phone later... Who may I say is calling? Burt Bacharach. Yes, thank you. Goodbye.

Pause. They look at each other. MARIA shakes her head.

MARLENE: What!

MARIA: I need to bath you. And change your sheets.

MARLENE: I don't want it now.

MARIA: I can't leave you with such disgusting sheets.

MARLENE: Yes, you said.

MARIA: How can I leave you?

MARLENE: Louis will come tomorrow.

MARIA: Will he?

MARLENE: I am never alone. I have my books, my films, my records. My letters. My phone. I have everything.

MARIA: But there's no-one to change your sheets.

MARLENE: I don't need it. I told you.

MARIA: You'll fester. I'm surprised you don't have lice.

MARLENE: I know about lice. In the war…

MARIA: No, don't start about the war! I need to talk about it. You'll start on the war and I'll never get to tell you

MARLENE: What?

MARIA: What I've come to tell you.

MARLENE: You want to tell me something?

MARIA: I've been trying to. You know what I want to tell you and you stop me, manipulate me, like you've always manipulated me. It's no good, Massy. This can't go on.

MARLENE: Kirk Douglas said he's coming to visit.

MARIA: Stop. Listen. I've arranged

MARLENE: I wish these people understood…a phone call is all I need. Why do they keep, pestering? They all want to come and see me. Let's go visit Marlene. We have nothing better to do!

MARIA: It's a really lovely

MARLENE: I suppose it's because, they want to see me,

MARIA: Place, the people there

MARLENE: To laugh at me now.

MARIA: Are kind. *(Pause.)* People don't laugh.

MARLENE: Look at her. Lying there so old.

MARIA: You're not so old. Anyway, this place, it's in the hills. Very exclusive. Very few people, the ratio of staff to

MARLENE: So, ugly!

MARIA: You're not ugly.

MARLENE: They want to feel superior. That is why they want to come. They want to see me so they feel better in themselves. Well, at least I don't look as bad as Marlene Dietrich. How the mighty have fallen!

MARIA: Stop feeling so sorry for yourself! And listen to me. I'm telling you about this place. My God, I can't believe you feel so sorry for yourself. If there's one person who's had her fair share

MARLENE: Had! The past doesn't count.

MARIA: Why doesn't it count? When does it stop counting? As soon as things go badly?

MARLENE: I can't live on past glories.

MARIA: But that's what you do!

MARLENE: No. I am still involved. I write letters to people I know, great people, important people. And they listen to me. I phone them, and they listen to me. Do you know why?

MARIA: Because you were Marlene Dietrich.

MARLENE: Because I *am* Marlene Dietrich.

MARIA: You see, you still have that fighting spirit. You carry on like that and you'll live to 120.

MARLENE: And that's supposed to comfort me?

Pause.

MARIA: Massy,

MARLENE: We were talking about you. Go on, about how you felt such rage. Tell me. I want to know.

MARIA: Amazing how you always manage to do it.

MARLENE: I know how you went through that period of mishigas

MARIA: Mishigas?

MARLENE: Yes. Everyone has a period of mishigas. No?

MARIA: *(Softly.)* Thank God for Bill.

MARLENE: Was hast Du gesagt?

MARIA: Yes, everyone has...

MARLENE: In those days I was so madly in love with Gabin. I loved Gabin. I still love him.

MARIA: He was, very lovable.

MARLENE: Yes!

MARIA: He and I, we got on very well, you know, a real warmth. He was different from the others, didn't involve me in his passion. Didn't tell me how much he adored my mother. I appreciated...

MARLENE: Why didn't you want to hear about how much they loved me.

MARIA: Surprising, no?

MARLENE: You sound like me now!

MARIA: Do I?

MARLENE: Did I know Charles Boyer, sweetheart?

MARIA: You were with him in The Garden of Allah.

MARLENE: Terrible film. What rubbish that was.

Why did I forget him? I am becoming old and ill.

MARIA: Look, as I was saying, that's what I want to... I'm trying to tell you

MARLENE: You do know I always loved you more than life itself.

MARIA: Don't start that again.

MARLENE: It's true.

MARIA: You've always said it. You've never shown it.

MARLENE: But I'm always phoning you.

MARIA: You are. And that shows, what exactly?

MARLENE: That I need you. I always needed you. I always
said, get Maria, she's the only one who knows how to do
this, or that. You even taped my breasts up

MARIA: From the age of eleven!

MARLENE: Exactly, even as a little girl, in the studio, on the
set, get Maria, she can do this. She can do that.

MARIA: Yes. But you wouldn't help yourself. I tried to stop you
drinking

MARLENE: and I always gave you, everything, look at your
house, things, I always made sure you had, you were never
short. You needed something, who gave it to you. Look
at when the boys were born, well Michael anyway, how I
came, looked after that boy while you and Bill went away
for the summer. Spent the whole time cleaning, looking
after him

MARIA: It was five days.

MARLENE: What was five days?

MARIA: You had him for five days

MARLENE: I would have had him for more. I put myself at
your entire disposal.

MARIA: We only needed you for five days.

MARLENE: Well I was available.

MARIA: Our apartment wasn't good enough so you borrowed
a friend's house, went there with your Lysol and Ajax like
weapons in holsters. Everything was washed, scrubbed,

polished. The room he was in was like a ward, intensive care, sterile. You ordered a nurse's uniform.

MARLENE: Well

MARIA: You wanted to look the part, I know.

MARLENE: It suited me, no?

MARIA: And our little baby was taken from his sweet, *clean*, nursery, to your surgical

MARLENE: Imagine if something had happened while I was looking after him. I hardly slept the whole time, kept listening to make sure he was still breathing.

MARIA: You hardly touched him.

MARLENE: Well, you used to hold him so much.

MARIA: And why not?

MARLENE: It's not good for a baby. Germs.

MARIA: By the time we came back, you'd

MARLENE: I did not.

MARIA: Yes you had. You'd convinced yourself, he was yours.

MARLENE: Kwatsch!

MARIA: And others too. People looked at me, askance. How could you have just torn the baby out of your mother's arms. She, who had cared for him, mothered him, for a whole year!

MARLENE: Such exaggeration!

MARIA: Exaggeration? Ha! You used to tell Michael I'd deserted him. Beaten him.

MARLENE: Nonsense.

MARIA: When he was little. That you'd been his only hope!

MARLENE: I don't know why you say such things.

MARIA: When he was older, he asked me why I used to beat him as a baby. My jaw dropped, I couldn't believe what I was hearing. He realized the truth when he saw my look.

MARLENE: People remember what they want to remember. You suggest that I was cruel

MARIA: No

MARLENE: Nasty. But I haven't a mean bone in my body.

MARIA: I'm not saying

MARLENE: All I did, I did from love. The problem is I always loved you, but you, you...

Pause.

MARIA: Oh Massy, am I getting

MARLENE: What?

MARIA: I don't mean to be so,

MARLENE: You always find fault.

MARIA: Angry.

MARLENE: I lie here, all alone. Lonely, waiting for my daughter to come and then you just

MARIA: I try and

MARLENE: Control yourself?

MARIA: I try.

MARLENE: That is sad, no?

MARIA: It's not that I don't

MARLENE: Do you?

MARIA: I see you as I see you, Massy.

MARLENE: Kwatsch!

MARIA: Ok, kwatsch.

MARLENE: I am more forgiving. I see you as a beautiful woman, a wonderful mother and wife, a great actress who gave up her career.

MARIA: And you think, idiot. Fool, waste of a life. How could I give up my career when

MARLENE: It was going so well. You were well known. You did so many television films, and then travelling with that wonderful theatre company. You were very talented. And you were becoming famous in your own right, not because you were my daughter.

MARIA: I got the roles because I was your daughter.

MARLENE: Only at the beginning.

MARIA: I never used your name. Or Papi's.

MARLENE: Remember that picture on the front page of Life magazine. You were on top looking down and I was at the bottom looking up. You see. I was looking up. At you. It was as if, you were the future and I... . You had the world, well almost at your feet. A bit longer, a few more films. You could've had it all. Everything I had.

MARIA: No, never.

MARLENE: You could've! You should have. You were my successor. You were the one who was supposed to carry on. You were never as beautiful but with good lighting, diets. You were there from the beginning, learning at my feet. What better chance was there and you just threw it away! And for what?

MARIA: For what? For normality. For reality. I didn't want to be you! I never wanted to be you!

MARLENE: But why not?

MARIA: Because... Massy, don't you understand?

MARLENE: Why wouldn't you want to be me?

MARIA: Because I wanted to be normal.

MARLENE: Normal is just another word for insignificant. For average, for ordinary.

MARIA: Yes. Ordinary. Normal person and normal family. That all-American family Jack and Rosemary had. I'd never had a family.

MARLENE: How can you say that!

MARIA: Ours was so abnormal.

MARLENE: Papi, me, all those wonderful people

MARIA: Do you know who was the only one I really felt...

MARLENE: Felt what?

MARIA: Who really felt like…

MARLENE: What are you saying?

MARIA: The only one who ever felt like a truly loving parent.

MARLENE: That ridiculous woman again.

MARIA: She was so gentle, so sweet. So kind.

MARLENE: A lunatic.

MARIA: You made her into a lunatic. You and Papi. You did it. All those treatments, those terrible electro shock treatments. All she wanted was to have a baby! And you made her have abortions.

MARLENE: I did not.

MARIA: Papi did, you did. It's all the same. The lie had to carry on, that he was your husband. If she'd had a baby, it would have all come out. Dietrich's husband fathers another woman's child. How would that look for the great Marlene Dietrich!

Can you imagine what it was like to be her. Always in the shadows. Always grateful to you for the hand-me-downs, the favours, being allowed to tag along. Having to have her own room so that no-one could know she slept in Papi's. Being at the receiving end of Papi's temper, not temper so much, more, sarcasm, patronising, he was so patronising to her. *You* were so patronising to her. She was so frightened all the time. Yes, it was Papi's temper. He was so strict with her, like a child, and once, once she'd bought a piece of meat for him and during the meal he shouted, this meat is terrible, how much did you pay for it, right, take it straight back to the butcher's and demand your money back, now! And he made her get up, she was shaking, trembling and she took the meat, the cooked, half eaten meat, in the middle of the meal, and went to the butcher's, crying, sobbing. I can't bear to think about it now.

MARLENE: She should've bought a good piece of meat.

MARIA: That's it? That's all you can say? She should've bought better meat? Not Papi shouldn't have been such a brute! He was a bully and nasty and horrible to her. Why will you never say anything against Papi?

MARLENE: He was my husband until he died.

MARIA: In name only.

MARLENE: He stood by me all those years. Papilein. He supported me, helped me, loved me. I could always call on him and he would come running. No?

MARIA: Lots of men did. And women. All your lovers did.

MARLENE: But he did it all his life.

MARIA: You supported him just as much.

MARLENE: I support all of you. Everyone depends on me.

MARIA: Bill makes a fine living, thank you Massy, and you know it.

MARLENE: I bought you your first house.

MARIA: Yes. We all know that. We all know how grateful we must be to Marlene Dietrich.

MARLENE: I always give. I always have. And not only material things. If anyone of my friends is ill, I go to them and cook, and clean and sit with them. All night, I sit with them. And help them. And even when they don't need help I still go to them, and clean. Me, with my Ajax and my rubber gloves, I vacuum, and scrub and clean.

MARIA: But Massy

MARLENE: What? But! You know I do it.

MARIA: Yes, you do! You go to their houses and you clean and you vacuum and you scrub, but don't you realize when you do that, what you're saying to them?

MARLENE: That I love them. That I will give of myself.

MARIA: That their houses are dirty.

MARLENE: Kwatsch!

MARIA: You insult them!

MARLENE: That is the most ridiculous thing I have ever heard in my life!

Pause.

MARLENE puts on some of her music. She sings along to it, and drinks some more. MARIA takes her glass off her and drinks from it.

MARLENE: *(Maudlin.)* Do you remember how they loved me in Israel. They warned me before, don't sing in German, but I said to the audience, shall I sing to you in German, and they all shouted, yes! I took German back to them. I made them accept again... Me, I made them accept my language. Their language. *(Starting to be very upset/cry.)* How they suffered. But they trusted me. They knew Hitler tried to get me to go back to Germany. That he offered me the moon, but I laughed in his face, ha ha, I laughed *(Crying now.)* ha ha

Pause.

MARIA: Massy. Come, look at me, now tell me, which is your absolute all-time favourite picture?

MARLENE: *(Getting a grip.)* You mean, still or movie?

MARIA: Still.

MARLENE: You know which it is.

MARIA: Scarlet Empress, the one with the bottle green

MARLENE: velvet. And the fur was

MARIA: Mink

MARLENE: The handmuffs

MARIA: were so wide they

MARLENE: spread from one end of the body to the other.

MARIA: And the hat tilted

MARLENE: to form a perfect counterbalance to the shape of my head.

MARIA: The collar opened

MARLENE: slightly

MARIA: to form a v

MARLENE: that directly reflected the two big v shapes

MARIA: on the skirt.

MARLENE: That was for reviewing the troops.

MARIA: I loved the way the horses ran up those steps.

MARLENE: Von Sternberg was, a genius. I should have loved him more. He was so passionate. I couldn't cope with all that passion.

MARIA: He couldn't cope with all the rivals.

MARLENE: Papi always could. Right from the beginning. As soon as you were born, he knew he would always share me

MARIA: He was always there.

MARLENE: Always. You must remember that about him, sweetheart. He will always be your father.

MARIA: He was a pathetic

MARLENE: He was not! Don't say that. He was cultured, smart, loving.

MARIA: To you.

MARLENE: Naturlich.

MARIA: He had these ridiculous pretensions.

MARLENE: Not really

MARIA: Do you remember, the bread.

MARLENE: The bread. Well, he knew what bread he wanted with his borscht

MARIA: *(Imitating Papi with controlled fury.)* 'Where is the black bread?'

MARLENE: *(Imitating a head waiter in distress.)* Oh Monsieur Sieber, a million apologies, this morning our baker,

MARIA: *(Continues imitation.)* such a good man, such a beautiful wife

MARLENE: from Odessa,

MARIA: she died

MARLENE: while giving birth

MARIA: *(As PAPI.)* 'You have served borscht without black bread!'

And then he marched us out without eating. And I was starving!

They laugh.

MARLENE: You see, we can always laugh together. It's better than being angry, nicht?

MARIA: There was fun too.

MARLENE: Of course there was.

MARIA: Shall I make something to eat?

MARLENE: I can make it. What would you like? I know what I want

And she pours a whisky. Maria goes to pour some water and as she does this, Marlene pops some pills.

MARIA: Massy, you know that I know that every time I try to talk to you about what I need to talk about, you very skilfully

MARLENE: I know what you want to talk about.

MARIA: Good. So let's talk about it now.

MARLENE: You want to talk about, the Proust reader!

MARIA: The what?

MARLENE: He does a documentary about me, and to prepare to talk to a movie star, Maximillian Schell has to read Proust.

MARIA: I do need to talk to you about the documentary, but

MARLENE: Ehrlich. You know what it is, don't you?

MARIA: What?

MARLENE: Mishigas!

MARIA laughs.

MARLENE: You showed it to me. I told you what I think about it. I can't believe that you can think that junk is any good. It's horrible, terrible. Absolute crap.

MARIA: Massy!

MARLENE: There's no other word for it. And everyone is saying it's so good. You say it's good. What's good about it? He uses other people to pretend it was me speaking.

MARIA: That is not true and you know it!

MARLENE: I would never have said half the things he says I did.

MARIA: It was your voice.

MARLENE: I was not so vulgar. I am not vulgar.

MARIA: You said so many ridiculous things.

MARLENE: Like what?

MARIA: That you didn't have a sister.

MARLENE: I said I didn't have a sister?

MARIA: Yes!

MARLENE: They must have faked my voice. I'm suing them.

MARIA: Why would you say you didn't have a sister?

MARLENE: Exactly.

MARIA: But you did!

MARLENE: I know I did. Elisabeth.

MARIA: But you said you didn't.

MARLENE: Did, didn't. This is all becoming ridiculous. I don't know what you're talking about, Maria. It's very tiring hearing you say did didn't.

MARIA: Look, the main thing is that you're now trying to sue them. I've been in touch with your German lawyers

MARLENE: Those ones I'm going to fire. I've been speaking to a different one.

MARIA: But Massy, the cost! And for what?

MARLENE: I don't want to talk to you about it. It's up to me and I will do it.

MARIA: You don't have a leg to stand on. Ooh, sorry… .That wasn't the best

MARLENE: It's alright, sweetheart.

MARIA: Sometimes you say things that just don't bear any relation to reality. To what actually happened.

MARLENE: Kwatsch. Name me one thing.

MARIA: God! So many… . Like the time you decided to give up smoking because you'd finally been convinced it was bad for your circulation and necessary to save your legs.

MARLENE: Yes.

MARIA: But smoking was intrinsic to your sex appeal.

MARLENE: *(She simulates smoking and pulls in her cheeks.)*

MARIA: Yes, very sexy! But you had to explain to the world why this sex goddess had stopped smoking. So you simply got Noel involved.

MARLENE: You don't walk so well. We'll say we made a bet and

MARIA: whoever smokes loses.

MARLENE: *(As NOEL.)* Of course, I would *adore* a cigarette! But I simply *can't,* I have a bet on with Marlenah.

MARIA: And when he did start smoking again, years later, you were furious.

MARLENE: What about our bet!

MARIA: What bet? He said.

MARLENE: He lost the bet.

MARIA: There was no bet!

And what about the time you met George Bernard Shaw.

MARLENE: It was wonderful. That marvellous man. He was already old. His skin was, you know people who won't eat meat, all those vegetables give such an odd texture to the skin. I sat down at his feet. You know how I do that when I meet a wonderful man, and woman. We talked for hours until it was dark. He was brilliant but he had some strange ideas. I mean he liked Hitler, for God's sake. But he loved the Russians and we recited poems to each other. He was amazed at how many I knew by heart. You know I have a wonderful memory for poetry. I know so many.

MARIA: Papi had a different version.

MARLENE: Papi wasn't there.

MARIA: But of course you went back and told him what happened. That when you sat at his feet, you had to, crank him up, shall we say, before he would begin to recite any Russian poetry at all.

MARLENE: I don't know why men like it so much! I never did!

They both laugh.

MARLENE: Ach, sweetheart. I nearly forgot. I have something for you. It will make you a fortune when I die. I was going to post it to you but, well, here you are, so I can just give it

MARIA: What is it?

MARLENE: Well you know I was telling you that I am worried about AIDS.

MARIA: You are not going to get AIDS, Massy! Gosh, it's like that time you thought you were pregnant with Yul.

MARLENE: It wasn't impossible.

MARIA: You were over fifty. You were having your menopause.

MARLENE: Anyway, we're not talking about that. We're talking about AIDS and don't be so clever, because you don't know!

MARIA: So who're you sleeping with? Your old doctor crazy man in LA?

MARLENE: You don't only get it from sleeping with people. You can get it from opening letters from people with it.

MARIA: Who said so?

MARLENE: I know.

MARIA: Rubbish!

MARLENE: And how do you know you can't?

MARIA: It's nonsense.

MARLENE: Well you know I get so many fan letters from queers. Many of them have AIDS now. So I'm careful how I open letters now.

She digs in her papers and comes up with a piece of paper. It is a poem. She hands it to MARIA.

MARLENE: This is for you.

MARIA reads it. It is dreadful.

Thank you, Massy.

MARLENE: You're welcome. I have always provided for you. I will continue to do so in death!

MARIA: Stop.

MARLENE: You will inherit my medals when I die.

MARIA: You and your dying.

MARLENE: The Medal of Freedom, America's highest honour the nation can bestow on a civilian. And the Legion d'Honneur, for services to France.

MARLENE sings the Marseillaise.

MARLENE: I never felt so happy as in the army.

MARIA: I know.

MARLENE: Filthy, tired, but there I was in the middle of the war.

Hello boys. I hardly thought it was possible that entertainment of such high calibre could be presented out here in the field. If morale is kept as high such as I have seen during my visit here in Italy, I am certain we can look forward to a speedy victory. Good bye, good luck and God speed.

It was always, hello boys. Then good bye, good luck and God speed.

I used to sit on the chair at the end of the show, put my musical saw between my legs and play it!

MARIA: No wonder they loved you!

MARLENE: I'd get dressed, glittering, sparkling, no matter how cold, how muddy. I loved them.

MARIA: You certainly did!

MARLENE: Those poor boys, it might have been their last night on earth. If I could help, and some of them I helped even more than they could possibly have imagined!

We went all over, sweetheart. Camps set up just before a battle, improvised stages. Every day we moved from place to place, standing, performing for fifty, five thousand. I was worn out, dead beat, but I carried on, risking my life, fearing what could happen. Imagine if I'd been captured, what a triumph for them. The woman who refused Hitler. The woman who laughed in Hitler's face, rejected his offer to come back home to be the Nazi's great movie queen!

One night we got lost.

MARIA: I know this story.

MARLENE: We were in no man's land very close to the enemy. Our jeep had broken down.

MARIA: I know.

MARLENE: We lay all night curled up in our jeep, frozen, listening to the gunfire, frightened out of our lives. Luckily there was some alcohol to keep out the cold. And in the morning we were found by

MARIA/MARLENE: the Free French forces.

MARIA: Including the actor Jean-Pierre Aumont.

MARLENE: Yes. You do remember the story.

MARIA: Mmm.

MARLENE: The Generals were so worried for me

MARIA: You were fucking all the Generals!

MARLENE: You sound resentful. You think I'm exaggerating.

MARIA: Of course you're not exaggerating, but I know this, Massy. All my life you've told me. I've seen the pictures, I've watched the documentaries, I've got the t shirt!

MARLENE: Ja, well

MARIA: You weren't the only one!

MARLENE: I never said I was.

MARIA: But you were the one who got all the medals. Who everyone talked about. The heroine! She saved the world single handed!

MARLENE: Now you're being ridiculous.

MARIA: What about the others?

MARLENE: I didn't need to go. I could have stayed in Hollywood with my Rolls-Royces and my luxury. Instead I

MARIA: stayed in tents

MARLENE: Froze

MARIA: Ate what the men ate.

MARLENE: Had crabs. And not the ones you eat!

MARIA: You were very brave. We all know that! And yes, you did make an enormous contribution.

MARLENE: So, why are you suggesting I

MARIA: I'm not suggesting, I just want you to acknowledge

MARLENE: Acknowledge what?

MARIA: That you were only one of many.

MARLENE: To those boys who sat there knowing that tomorrow they may die, looking at me, at my beautiful legs tantalising them, teasing, provoking, alluring, I was not just one of many. I was Marlene Dietrich, and that was something they'd remember all their lives!

Pause.

MARLENE: I told you about the lovely cemetery I once found. It would have been so perfect. It was so near an excellent restaurant. You could have had lunch when you came to visit me.

MARIA: But you would have had to be French!

MARLENE: I've been making lists, important lists.

MARIA: Oh yes?

MARLENE: What needs to be done. I've been thinking, how to get me out, without being seen. We need something tough, no, that won't spill, or split. It would be so inconvenient if it suddenly split.

MARIA: You can't die here alone.

MARLENE: You know that Balenciaga raincoat I got in the fifties. The rubber is strong. The worms will never get through it. What you must do is wrap me in it, then use those strong black plastic bags, the heavy duty ones. Get Peter to help you, he's the strongest of your boys. Then you stuff me inside. Don't worry if you have to use force, you know, break anything, arms or, that's ok. Then take the elevator to the basement garage, put it in the car and then off to America, or anywhere.

MARIA: You aren't going to die here.

MARLENE: If I'd died when I was still beautiful, Paramount would have taken charge. They'd get my make-up and hair artists to come. How will we get those false eyelashes to stay on, they'd worry. What about her hair? They don't have to think about the back, just the front. Because I'll be lying on the back, you see. Papi will be there, organising it all. But, he can't now, can he? I had such plans. Should I use my foundation for the stage dress? Papi will say no. She needs to wear something simple, a simple black dress from Coco Chanel. Papi knows I always wanted to wear a simple black dress, like Piaf.

De Gaulle wants to bury me next to the Unknown Soldier at the Arc de Triomphe and the service must be at the Notre Dame. No, I want it at the Madeleine. We must think of the chauffeurs. They can have a coffee at Fauchon while they wait.

How will they move the body? Six black horses to pull the coffin, draped in the tricolor, made by Dior.

The queers have arrived from all over the world. The crowds weep as the coffin passes. In the meantime, the invited guests arrive at the church. Papi stands there greeting them. He has a special task. On a table in front of him are two boxes filled with carnations, white and red. As each guest enters the church, he gives him or her a carnation to wear, red for those who made it and white for those who say they slept with me but never did. Only Papi knows!

MARIA: You could have the entire 82ⁿᵈ Airborne Division with General Gavin, all wearing red carnations

MARLENE: Only two red carnations are left in the box. Remarque is lying in his bed unable to get up. And Gabin? He is leaning against a wall, blowing smoke from his cigarette into rings.

She is getting very tired.

Pause.

MARIA: It's not going to happen. Massy, you know it, don't you?

MARLENE: Of course.

MARIA: It's not possible to go on like this. Is it? You know that too, don't you?

MARLENE: What do you want?

MARIA: I've arranged a lovely place. Kind, gentle people. Quiet, very few, very select. They know, they understand. In the mountains. Nobody comes. You'll have your phone. Your newspapers. You can still contact anyone, everyone. Books. Television. Your records with the applause. No-one will take anything away from you. They'll just look after you. Give you proper meals, take you to the toilet, or at least give you a bed pan. That's easier than a Limoges vase. Isn't it? Be there when you're lonely, when nobody comes.

MARLENE: It sounds

MARIA: Idyllic.

MARLENE: Idyllic?

MARIA: Yes, doesn't it?

MARLENE: Yes.

MARIA: Oh thank goodness. Massy, I'm so relieved. I can't tell you how relieved I am! I was so worried after last time when I told you you had to, and you responded in such a, and then I left you to stew, and I just thought you would never, you wouldn't agree to it, but I knew you would eventually, if I just left you for a bit, until you, and you, because it's so sensible

MARLENE: Idyllic, but not for me.

MARIA: Not for you? What do you mean?

MARLENE: Me, now? With people coming and going, telling me what to do, looking at me and saying, do you know who she was? That used to be Marlene Dietrich.

MARIA: But you'll be looked after, safe.

MARLENE: I'll be looked *at*! They'll look at me. Don't you understand?

MARIA: Why does that matter now?

MARLENE: Because I will always be Marlene Dietrich. Until I die. And even then I will be Marlene Dietrich because that is all the world will know. That is what will continue, that will live forever. That image, that picture. The beauty. Not the old, haggard, concentration camp survivor!

MARIA: So, you won't.

MARLENE: I will die in this room. And no-one beyond you, Louis and the concierge, will ever see me.

Pause.

MARIA: I thought I could convince you. I thought just once, just this once towards the end of her life, she'll do what's right

MARLENE: By you?

MARIA: Not just by me! By you! You!

MARLENE: I know what is right...

MARIA: And so you think everything you've always done was right? Mrs Infallible. Mrs Never Fucking Wrong!

MARLENE: No, not everything. But it doesn't mean I'm consumed with remorse. There are far more things I don't regret. I don't regret the films I made with von Sternberg that are considered classics today. I don't regret the wonderful creations I made that shimmered and glittered and made people gasp. I don't regret all the men and women I slept with, not one single one of them. I don't regret the cabaret performances where people applauded and shouted and screamed for more. I don't regret the wonderful songs I sang

Go see what the boys in the back room will have
And tell them I'm having the same
Go see what the boys in the back room will have
And give them the poison they name
And when I die don't spend my
 money
On flowers in my picture in a frame
Just see what the boys in the back room will have
And tell them I sigh, and tell them I cry and tell them I
died of the same.

She is exhausted

MARLENE: Maria.

MARIA: Yes.

MARLENE: There is one thing I regret. I sometimes wonder whether anyone really loved me at all.

MARIA: How can you say that?

MARLENE: What did they love? The glamour, the fame, the beauty. Would they have loved me if I'd been Maria Magdalene, German hausfrau that once was something in silent films. Then suffered during the war and did her bit for the Winter fund and the Nazis, like all the other good German women. And married a dear little sausage maker from Bremen who did well after the war. Like so many others.

MARIA: But you weren't like so many others.

MARLENE: I regret not helping Tami. I should have said something to Papi...

MARIA: Yes.

MARLENE: He treated her like that because

MARIA: Because

MARLENE: He knew I expected him to.

Does that make me…

MARIA: What?

MARLENE: I never felt anything with any of them. I married Papi because he was beautiful.

Even you have never loved me.

MARIA: You phone. I come.

MARLENE: Is that love?

MARIA: What is it then?

MARLENE: Duty.

MARIA: I worry.

MARLENE: Is that love?

MARIA: I don't worry about the drunk in the street.

MARLENE: But you do worry about the drunk in the bed.

MARIA: What do you want me to say? That I thank God every day of my life that he gave me a mother who was one of the greatest sex symbols and beauties of her day. That she was surrounded all her adult life by the adoration and adulation of millions. That I was brought up with luxury that few in this world can even imagine, that I was never hungry, thirsty or homeless, or when I was it was my own doing, and absolutely not the fault of my mother.

MARLENE: I need you, Maria. You are the only one.

MARIA: I know. So I must carry on with the charade.

MARLENE: Do it for me.

MARIA: And me? I know what is right for you.

MARLENE: In your eyes, but not mine.

MARIA: If you don't go, I'll leave you. You know I can. This time I really won't come back. I'll let you stay and fester in your sheets.

MARLENE: That's alright.

MARIA: Why is it alright?

MARLENE: Because it is.

MARIA: Please! Do it for me!

MARLENE: I'm very tired.

She drinks more and takes a few more pills.

MARLENE: Sweetheart. I have a busy day tomorrow, all those letters and people to...

No, I don't, do I, Maria? I don't have a busy day. The fan mail is falling off, only some queers who still remember me, and some cinema buffs who think they have discovered Marlene Dietrich when they watch Blue Angel.

I don't have a busy day. Maybe Louis will come, because he is still my friend, and will respond after the fifth pleading phone message. And the doctor from California will phone because he is a little crazy and obsessed with the image of a woman who no longer exists.

But I do have my bottles. You won't find them all, empty them all down the sink, will you? Leave them for me, and the pills.

Don't let the world see me like this. It's all I have, what I was.

Ich muss schlafen, I can't keep my eyes open. You...

She falls asleep.

MARIA watches her. She covers her and makes sure she's comfortable. She looks at the bottles. She makes sure the hot plate is off. She kisses her mother.

The entryphone rings. She answers it.

MARIA: Hello?.... Who?... *(Changes into a quasi Spanish accent.)...* . No, I'm afraid you may not come up. Miss Dietrich regrets she is not available. She has gone out for the day but you may phone later... .Who may I say is calling? Kirk Douglas. Yes, thank you. Goodbye.

Blackout.

SHACKLETON'S CARPENTER

Shackleton's Carpenter produced by New Vic Productions in association with Eastbourne Theatres, 20 November 2014, Devonshire Park Theatre with the following cast:

HARRY MCNISH Malcolm Rennie

Director Tony Milner

Production Manager Paul Debreczeny

Stage Manager Lucy Myers

Black

Crackle of old radio. Broadcaster's voice:

BROADCASTER: And now over to our studio in Savoy Hill where Lieutenant General Sir Hastings Anderson will talk to us about Heroic Adventure.

LG SIR HA: The time of heroic adventure is a time that we need to refer back to now, a must in these times of austerity and depression. 1916, already fourteen years ago, Sir Ernest Shackleton returned to England after his ill-fated journey on the Endurance. It was August 1914 that Sir Ernest, together with 27 hand-picked men and 69 dogs, set out in the Endurance, to sail through the Weddell Sea with the aim of hitting land and walking across the Antarctica. But within only 80 miles of their destination, indeed, only one day's sailing, the Endurance became trapped in the ice and was unable to move.

For ten months the men waited for the ice to break and continue their journey. But finally the Endurance was crushed by the pressure of the ice and sank.

The men spent two days trying to walk across the ice floes, hills and valleys of ice, to reach open sea but they were forced to give up the impossible task. Six months they spent camping on the ice as it moved further and further away from the land.

When the ice had finally melted sufficiently for the men, now without their dogs, to sail away, they set out on three little open lifeboats and for seven days they sailed and finally succeeded in reaching the uninhabited Elephant Island.

From there, six of the men sailed in the James Caird. You might ask how a little lifeboat could survive fifteen days in a harrowing 600 mile journey through the worst seas on God's Earth. It was thanks not only to the leadership of Shackleton, the navigational brilliance of Frank Worsley but also to the skilful hands of Shackleton's carpenter, Harry McNish.

The six managed to reach South Georgia. However, after such tremendous difficulty and danger, they had arrived on the wrong side of the island and three of them had then to make a further harrowing journey on foot across the uncharted mountains of South Georgia, finally to reach help at the whale station Grytviken.

By the time the men were saved from Elephant Island, not one of the twenty eight men's lives had been lost.

Twenty four gallant men were awarded the distinctive Polar Medal. Those who did not were William Stephenson and Jack Vincent, both still working as seamen, Ernie Holness who died aged 31, washed overboard, and Harry McNish, Shackleton's carpenter, last seen living destitute on the wharf in Wellington New Zealand. It is not known at this stage whether McNish is alive or dead.

BROADCASTER: Thank you, Sir Hastings Anderson. And now over to Ambrose and his orchestra, coming to you from the ballroom of the May Fair Hotel...

Music.

MCNISH is asleep in his sleeping bag in a little lifeboat on board an old ship in Wellington harbour, New Zealand. It is the middle of the night, quiet, warmish. The boat has some tarpaulin covering it. His head is on a small kitbag and a few items can be seen stored neatly in the boat; a small primus stove, some cans of food, tea, a bottle of Scotch whiskey.

MCNISH's sleep is disturbed. He is dreaming that he is on board the James Caird, in the cabin below deck of the tiny boat that carried Shackleton and 5 of his crew from Elephant Island to South Georgia, across some of the most dangerous waters in the world. Below deck, three men could lie sardine fashion, sleeping on moving stones that served as ballast. It was dangerous and frightening and lying there felt a bit like drowning in a coffin.

MCNISH is dreaming that he is drowning in that cabin.

He wakes with a start and sits up coughing and spluttering.

Drowning. Coffin, sardines in a coffin.

He has to get up and move his legs. Nobody is around. It is 2 or 3 in the morning.

He feels terrible. He is clearly not well, and it doesn't help being in the open, on a cold night. He rubs himself, hugs himself, shakes himself. Sits down against the boat, then takes his stool, his primus, his little pot and boils some water.

As it boils he calls for his cat.

Mrs Chippy. Where are you?

He makes his tea in a little teapot, takes the scotch and pours some, a large dollop, into the mug. He drinks a large slurp from the bottle too.

Where's that cat, gone to the dogs, you gone to see the dogs, when you need him. Always around those dogs, teasing those, woof woof woof. Mrs Chippy, here, careful of all the ice, don't go off...no. Not Mrs ...here cat. Come here cat.

He finishes making his tea and drinks it, lighting up a fag or a pipe at the same time.

Early.

Dark.

Not well. Should sleep.

Suddenly sees someone approach.

Who's that? Who's there? There's someone there.

He drinks from the Scotch again.

He's gone. I could've sworn...

Drinks again.

Is that you, Sir Ernest? Is that you skulking round corners. Prying, spying. I know you're dead. You think you're going to haunt me?

You can't hurt me, you know. I don't care if you're dead.

You killed my cat. You shot Mrs Chippy. Poor defenceless little fellow. Just shot, like that. Didn't expect it. Trusted. What sort of man would just...

Lucky you're dead because if you weren't, I'd, give you a... I would, I swear. I'd lay into you. Don't care that you're the Boss. Anyway you're dead.

Come out of there. I can see you! What're you hiding from? Scared? Are you scared?

Nobody's there.

He gets up and goes to the water's edge.

Dark.

The colour of the berg just under the water, aquamarine. Pale, light, deep, dark, bright. Blue.

No green, no red, no orange. Blue. White. Black. Black for months, just that hint of light in the hours around noon. Then black, dark. Nothing.

Towers and domes in the Antarctic sky, mirages, but we swore they were true, white and gold, pictures from a child's story book. Billowing seas of ice, icebergs that weren't icebergs, ghostly icebergs, upside down on the horizon.

Quiet. The bangs of the floes cracking, pushing, piling high like boulders, groaning against each other. Difficult when we walked, with the dogs across the floes, woof woof woof woof, over the hills of ice, piling one up against another like, sea defences, boulders piling against each other, one on top, not planned, like God chucked all his toys out and they fell, one against another, on top, next to, against…

God doesn't have toys.

Apart from us. Play with. Discard. Let's see how they manage, see if they can manage, alone, just twenty eight, nobody else in all the space, all the whiteness, blue, aquamarine, under the icebergs. They'll go crazy. They'll eat each other. Won't take long before they're insane. Mad.

But no, we didn't go mad. Discipline. Order. *(Puts on Shackleton's voice.)* Everyone has a job and everyone knows what to do. We will get out of this alive. We will survive.

What was that? Is it you? Where are you? You came once before. On a night just like this. In darkness, in silence. Standing on the deck with nothing around, no-one, soulless, empty, alone. Just ice and snow and sky somewhere up above but never sure where it is, up there, amongst the stars, a heaven somewhere, but too far, too, away. I was alone in the midst of a whole world of nothing, nothing in the wild mass of space and foreverness, I stood alone. Nobody and nothing around me, within me, under me, above me. Alone and empty. Ready to leave, to stop, to go, to move on. Shaking and shivering, feverish and sweating, I stood. And then I saw you. A light near the horizon, somewhere there near the horizon, if I had been able to see the horizon. How can there be a light near the horizon where there is no-one? What can it be, who is able to walk in the freezing ice, coming closer and closer, moving swiftly towards me bearing a light. What force is it that comes to get me, on a night just like this. I could have run down to the bowels of the ship, woken the others, wake up, wake up, something comes, a light comes, what can it be. But I stop and I wait and I watch as the light gets closer and closer towards me. Who carries a light in the middle of nowhere? How does the light move with no-one there to carry it.

He suddenly notices Shackleton standing next to him. He's shocked.

Oh, you gave me a start. You just crept up on me. You always did that, creep up on people. Why don't you announce yourself? It is I, Sir Ernest Shackleton. Put down the red carpet. I have come to bestow upon you a visit. A visitation.

Why did you hold back? Did you think you wouldn't be welcome? Why wouldn't I welcome you, the Boss? It's an honour. I'm, delighted, I'm sure.

Anyway, anyone can walk along this wharf. It's not mine. I don't even pay rent. Rent free, this lifeboat. They even provide the tarpaulin.

You shot my cat.

You got nothing to say?

You shot the dogs. Sixty nine dogs, bang bang bang. The puppies. Creen's puppies. Sallie's little babies. So small. Who kills puppies. We all loved them. Not Lees. He never liked anything, never cared for anyone, anything, not my Mrs Chippy. Get her out of here, he shouted. He didn't even know Mrs Chippy was a he. But Mrs Chippy knew to avoid Lees' boots. I saw it, how he kicked at him but my cat swerved away, avoided him, knew instinctively who to trust. He trusted you. Never saw you as a bad 'un, someone to avoid. Thought he was safe with you.

'He couldn't have survived in the boats.'

I would've looked after him in the boats.

'I had to.'

No, you didn't have to. Of course, you say you had to. Just like you had to take the boats across the floes on sledges. We can do it, you said. 'For sudden the worst turns the best to the brave'. Browning you said. I knew we couldn't. It'll break up the lifeboats and then where will we be? Stuck on an ice floe, twenty eight people, ice breaking up, ice collapsing all around, sea getting nearer, nearer. Land hundreds of miles away. No boats. Twenty eight people, no boats.

Tell me I was right. You never said I was right.'You shouldn't've challenged me'. No. No-one must challenge the Boss.

'It was life and death out there. We couldn't have insubordination.'

Insubordination. That's what it's called. That's the posh for I'm the boss and you're just the skivvy. So shut yer gob.

What's it like to be dead, Sir Ernest?

Anyway, what're you doing down here? Shouldn't you be, stuck in one place. Is your soul still roaming, looking for adventure. Even dead you can't rest. Or have you escaped from hell? Too hot down there, need somewhere cool, somewhere cold, some ice, some floes, some bergs. Aquamarine bergs.

You come to keep me company? What? You're surprised to find me here, on this wharf? Oh, it's sleeping in this little boat, is it? You think I should be in a room, in a bed, a warm bed with a nice warm body beside me. You come to tell me what I should be doing. Who I should be sleeping with? You think you can come and keep me company and tell me what I should do. Order me around. Ask me questions? I'm not asking you questions, am I? I don't want to know why you couldn't stay at home with your lovely wife, your lovely children, your lovely house, all those riches, all those luxuries.

I'm not asking why you had to go off again on another 'adventure'. Back to the South when you knew you were ill, and you didn't even know what you were going for. Only that you had to go back. No. I'm not. You don't ask me and I won't ask you. Alright?

I heard you died in South Georgia. Had a heart attack and died. Didn't manage to get further south. The Quest, wasn't it, the name of your third boat, the next adventure. The last adventure, as it happened. They were going to send your body home for burial and your wife stopped them. Bury him there in South Georgia, she said. Maybe she thought you wouldn't roam again if you were left there, that you'd feel at home amongst the snow and the ice and the cold.

But here you are. Does she know? Have you been to see her? Haunted her. Ghosts can travel, can't they? You've come all the way from South Georgia to New Zealand. You could've stopped off in London for a bit. I know it's out of the way but how long does it take to travel when you're a ghost? Is it in the blink of an eye or is it true time. Is that why you've just got here now? Did you hitch a ride on a boat? Where do you sleep as a ghost? Kip in with the skipper, or down in the hold amongst the coal, afraid to be discovered, to frighten, to be a stowaway. No, even as a ghost you're going to push that captain to the side and get in there right next to him. Where you belong. Your sort. Your class.

Blackborow was a stowaway. Got the fright of your life when you saw a stowaway on board. Gave him the fright of his life. 'Do you know that on these expeditions we often get very hungry, and if there is a stowaway available he is the first to be eaten,' you yelled at him. And his reply – 'They'd get a lot more meat off you, sir.' Well you were a stocky, well-fed fellow, weren't you. You had the grace to laugh.

She must be alive still, your wife. She's young, your age, isn't she? And you're mine. You always spoke about me as the old carpenter. But I was always seven months younger than you. Well, I was. Until you died.

What's it like, death? Is it like those days and nights in the dark in the winter waiting for the sun to appear, waiting four months, six months for real daylight. And then it comes, how it comes, non stop, light, but now you want some darkness to sleep with, to befriend you, at night, to help you sleep.

Is it like that, death. Why won't you let yourself just sleep?

I like it here, on this wharf, in this lifeboat. I'm my own
boss, here. No-one to tell me what to do, to order me
about, to tell me to take the boats across the floes when I
know that's wrong.

I tried to imagine what it was like to be dead when I was
little, in my bed, our bed, me and my brothers. We'd lie
there like sardines, on our sides, unable to move, unless
we all moved, ready boys, now, go, and we'd move. You
can't imagine what it's like to be dead if you're lying on
your side. You don't get buried on your side. You have to
be lying on your back, but you couldn't in the bed, with all
my brothers. There wasn't the space.

We didn't want to imagine what it was like to be dead
in the James Caird. It was too real, too possible. But we
dreamt it, lying in the cabin, sardines, on our sides, next
to each other, three at a time, three above sailing the
boat, watching, slashing at the ice, bailing out the water,
half a pint of water to drink each per day. Three below
sleeping, dreaming of dying, of drowning. The worst seas
in the world. Sixty foot waves, hundred foot waves. Three
thousand foot waves. Lying there on the shifting ballast,
knowing this could be your coffin, as you slip, as you
drown, as you die.

Here, have some whiskey? Can you drink? Do ghosts
drink? Do they eat? I've got some soup, can of soup. Sorry,
no seal liver. No penguins on the menu tonight. You've got
to warn me you're coming. Tell me next time and I'll get
some in. Nothing too good for the Boss.

Alright I'll tell you why I'm here. You insist on knowing,
you plague me with your questions. Tell me, tell me. Well
I'm here because, I like it, because I, because, where else
am I going to go. I've nowhere else to go. Look at my
hands. Look how gnarled, how painful. You want to shake
hands. No. I won't shake hands with you, with anyone.
I can't shake hands. My hands got destroyed over there
in the seas, on the floes, in the ice. How can I work with

hands like these? All they're good for now is to light the primus, lay out the sleeping bag, open a can of soup. Roll some baccy.

My hands were my, what, my fortune, my livelihood, my everything. You knew I was a brilliant carpenter, brilliant shipwright. McLeod, my pal knew it. Everyone knew it. Even Lees who hated me said I was brilliant. He doesn't even have to measure, they all say. Just looks at it, cuts, and it always comes out right. Make me a chest of drawers, cubicles, cofferdams, can you do instrument cases, Hussey says, specimen shelves, Clarke says, windscreens. Of course I can. That's what I do. Sailing beams, attending the boats, everything, anything with wood or iron. Inventive, creative, scavenging to find things to use to make things we need. Working all the time. Three days off the whole ten months the Endurance was stuck in the ice. You yourself said we couldn't have lived through the voyage without the changes I made to our lifeboat, our James Caird. No-one more deserves recognition than the old carpenter, Dr Macklin said. Old carpenter! There it is again, you see. What was it about those people! I was only forty. Seven months younger than you. Did they talk of the *old* Boss, the *old* Shackleton. It was the dynamic Boss, the inspiring Shackleton. The heroic adventurer. But McNish was always the old carpenter.

We sit on our boat, day in, day out, night in, night out, day in again, again. Keep active, keep busy, or we'll go mad.

I saw a light. Did I tell you? It came far off from the horizon. I sat watching as it came closer and closer. I could have gone to call you, but I was transfixed. And when it reached me,

Listen, can you hear that noise, it's the pressure of the ice. Listen, listen don't talk and you'll hear. Bang! Crash! Phaahhh!

Wait, what's that. A bit of sea, a crack in the ice, a lead of free water, ahead of us. Only 400 feet ahead, we can do

it, we can cut a path, get into that beautiful clear water
straight ahead of us, and on, away. Quick everyone down
there, get going, picks, shovels, anything, dig, dig, get a
path for our boat, shake the Endurance, shake it free, we
can do it, just dig, dig. Dig.

No, we can't. The ice is too thick, too powerful against the
picks and the shovels and the little men.

That noise, it never leaves me. Powww.

The pressure crashes our poor Endurance, snapping
the beams like match sticks, crunching it like a giant fist
destroying a discarded matchbox. We watch as our boat,
a ghostly semblance of a once boat, lies broken, shattered,
dying. It's going boys. Listen to it moan, hear it fight,
it's resisting what it knows is waiting for it, a cold black
grave. Look, those Emperor penguins over there, how
many, one, two, three, four, five, six, seven, eight. Eight
Emperor penguins watching the boat, like sirens, like
ghosts themselves from the underworld. How solemn they
are. Look at them as they watch. They throw their heads
back. That sound they make. Arrrgggghhhhh *(Emulating
the sound)*. It's unnerving, supernatural. They're singing the
ship's dirge. We'll none of us get back to our homes now,
McLeod says.

What the ice gets, the ice keeps.

When the light reached me, it took me, enfolded me,
engulfed me in its warmth, in its blueness, in its light, in its
life.

I hated Lees too. It was mutual. But most of us hated Lees,
the 'Colonel'.

You remember Boss, you remember what Worsley
wrote, facetiously, sarcastically. Sounds of bitter sobs and
lamentations from number five tent at the loss of the dearly
beloved Colonel, something like that, because he went
out, slept somewhere else. You let Lees go, you, always
fair, always making sure no-one was driven out, kicked

out. Because you knew he was hated. Fussy, worrying. Pessimistic. That was the worst, wasn't it, Boss. That's what you couldn't take at all. Everyone had to be optimistic. Like you. It's the worst sin. The sin of all sins. You can't be pessimistic. Drag the men down with pessimism.

But I was right about those boats, dragging those boats on the floes, destroying our boats. 'You were pessimistic!' I was pessimistic? So you shout at me, slate me, argue, make me feel five, six, a boy, a little boy, not a man. And you stop me from getting the polar medal. Why? Because I disagree with you, or because I'm, pessimistic.

What do you call a pessimist who is right?

You knew it two days later. 'You were right, Chippy. You understood before I did. You got it'. No, I don't even hear those words from you now.

Have a drink, Sir Ernest. Warm the cockles. Drink to drown out the, everything.

Hey, Mrs Chippy! Where are you? Come meet an old friend. Don't worry, you're alright. Ghosts don't carry guns.

He coughs and splutters and is clearly in pain.

It's alright. Don't worry. I'll be alright. Just the old problem of piles again, and other things, who knows. I'll be alright. Sit. Don't get up. I don't need anything. I'll have my tea.

He pours more Scotch in it. Offers Shackleton.

Are you sure?

Piles. Do you suffer from them? Did you? I've always suffered terribly. Have you ever? It's so, great big bunches of grapes up your arse. And that's not foul language. Except grapes are soft and can squash, and these are hard and they dig into you and press and pulsate and…

You had Sciatica. Yes, that was your problem. You couldn't move with Sciatica. The boys had to bring your food to you. You couldn't get up. Weeks you'd be gone with Sciatica. Even on the lifeboat you had Sciatica. How did you manage on that boat, three weeks on that boat, seven days in open sea, all the time suffering with Sciatica. People can't move but you sat, upright, awake, aware, come on, lads, you're doing well, lads, you can do it, we can do. We will do it.

What happens actually, when you have Sciatica? I've developed an interest in medical conditions. It's one of the things I think about as I lay here under the tarpaulin at night. Sciatica. Heart attack. Diphtheria, scarlet fever. Influenza.

I bet you wished now you'd had more religious services on that boat, hey, Sir Ernest! What happened when you faced St Peter? Did he ask you about it, did he question why you never had any religious services on your boat since the second out from Plymouth. Why you allowed such foul language on your boat. What did you say? What was your excuse? Maybe that's why you're still roaming. He didn't allow you in. No services down below, no service upstairs.

I'd never heard such filthy language, not before, not since. No religious service but filthy remarks. And of course they think it makes them manly instead of blackguards.

We used to discuss it, McLeod and me. We went for walks on the ice. And on the boat, he'd sit with me when I was watchman, once we'd got stuck, weren't moving anymore. He'd sit with me and we'd talk. I suppose you looked at us, two Scotsmen, two seamen, sitting round the fire, talking, drinking. What've they got in common, you thought, other than that they're Scottish, the old carpenter and the young able seaman. There you are you see, he was born in 1873 and I was born in 1874. So he was older than me. Did you talk of the old seaman? No! Only the old carpenter.

We sit round the stove, trying to stay warm as we keep an eye out on the ice, on the pressure. Did you hear something? Was that crack worse than the others? We'd go back to the Clyde, the harbour, the hills, the fields. We speak the same language, understand without explanation. Do you know anything about him? Did you ever find out where he was from, what he was, before he became one of your boys. Oh yes, you brought us tea as we lay in our tents on the ice. Early morning service, wake up, rise and shine. Tea for the boys. Yes, I did appreciate it. I know I never said it at the time, none of us did, but I did appreci... You were generous. I know that. You gave Wild your last biscuit the time before, on the Nimrod expedition, when there was nothing. All the money that was ever minted would not have bought that biscuit and the remembrance of that sacrifice will never leave me. That's what Wild said.

Would I give my last biscuit to a friend?

We sit thinking of food. We drool talking about how they look, how they're made. Sausages and mash, scones with jam and cream, fried kipper, fish and chips. The best meal we've ever had, the first meal we're going to have when we got back to civilisation. Hunger gnaws at us, acid rises looking searching for something, anything to get its teeth into. But we always do have something, we always do have just enough to keep us going. You make sure nobody starves.

Would I give my last biscuit?

You did. Why wouldn't I?

I had to fight for my share, with ten brothers and sisters and little money, you would, wouldn't you. You never had to fight for your share. Yours came on silver platters, with servants to place the delicate tasty morsels on your china plate. Would you like some more, sir. Have some more darling. Eat your fill. Shall we have wine. There's a delightful little 1900 in our wine cellar. It has a stunning bouquet. Marvellous colour, deep red, purple almost.

Lafitte Rothschild. *(Laughs.)* 'How do you know that?'
How does the old carpenter know about Lafitte Rothschild
1900. That sort of knowledge isn't for his class. What is the
world coming to if old carpenters from Port Glasgow know
about things like Lafitte Rothschild. Well I can put you out
of your misery. I'll tell you. It was the Colonel, Orde Lees.
That's how I know. He spoke about Lafitte Rothschild
1900. When we were discussing sausage and mash, he
would talk of the colour of the wine.

You made him scrub the floors, just like all the rest of us.

'I am able to put aside pride of caste in most things but I
think scrubbing floors is not fair work for people who have
been brought up in refinement.' (*Laughs).* He wrote that
in his diary. Yes, we all knew what people wrote in their
diaries, well Lees' anyway. Fair game. Some of us were just
more canny about what we wrote in ours.

What I don't understand about you is how you are part of
the boys and yet so far apart. You're the Boss. To everyone
you're the Boss. And yet you bring them tea, you laugh
with them, play football. You're one of them. But never
quite one of them. When we finally got back to civilisation,
to Buenos Aires, we men had to find and pay for our own
passage home, but you, the officers and scientists, were
given a liner to sail you back to London in luxury.

They all looked up to you. Admired you. Some of
them loved you. You were the Boss. You were not to be
challenged. No one did challenge you. No one questioned
your authority. You were God. Apart from me. I am the
only one who openly says to you, you're wrong.

I know. I understand. You don't have to tell me. It was
the times, the danger we're in. We have to listen. We can't
be divided. We're the parts and you're the driver, and
if one part falls off the whole thing disintegrates. Risks
disintegrating. I know that. Do you think I don't? I'm no
fool. But what must a man do when he knows the order
he's been given is wrong. Carry those boats over the floes.

'They're on sleds, it'll be alright, it'll be fine.' But we're risking breaking them and then where will we be! Look round, there's nothing. We're stuck here in the middle of the Weddell Sea with nothing. No means of escape. No-one knows we're here, that we're even alive. We'll stay here, rot here, die here.

Let me use the wood to build a sloop. 'No'. The noise is ice, pressure. 'No, it's a whale looking for a breathing place'. Let's wait for the floes to break up. 'No, we must walk, we must move on. People will go insane if they just sit, immobile, waiting, hungry, nothing to do'.

We should have built a sloop. The noise was the ice, the pressure, we should've waited for the floes to break up. But I am just Chippy the carpenter. And you are Sir Ernest Shackleton, polar explorer, hero of our age. Boss.

Six months we wait, camping on the ice. We don't go mad. 'That's because as the leader I enforce discipline, give you jobs, make sure we have our seal liver and seal steaks and penguin. Our milk powder, our preserved meat. Our jokes, our sing-songs. Our optimism.'

Our toasts on Saturdays nights to sweethearts and wives.

No don't ask me about that. I don't want to talk about that.

You talk about it. You tell me about your wife. Go on. What happened? Did you go back to her or to your mistress. I heard she was American, your mistress. What does she look like? Is she beautiful? Did they know each other? Is that why your wife wanted you buried in South Georgia? Keep you away from your mistress. If you're in South Georgia she can't exactly nip over to cry on your grave.

Why are you buried in Grytviken? It's the most disgustingly smelly place this side of the universe. The slush of whale blubber, blood, bones, smell of putrefying whale. Small, grey houses, great men whale men, shouting, swearing. You could snuff the aroma if you were five miles out to windward.

'The views'. Oh, the views, is it? Alright. They were extraordinary, that's true. As long as your grave is looking out to sea.

Do they come and pay homage at the grave of the great explorer? Or are you forgotten. What is that pile of old stones up there? A grave? Whose? Shackle-what? Never heard of him. Oh, wasn't he the one who went to the Antarctic with the old carpenter...

You haven't told me. Who did you choose?

I don't know what happened when I got back. You toast them, sweethearts and wives, you think about them, yearn for them. You dream of them when you lie in your sleeping bag. You can feel them, their touch, their breath. You stroke their hair, their faces, their breasts. They are with you as you sleep, they are with you at moments of quiet in the midst of the ice and the snow. They become the innermost part of you. You revere them, you immortalise them, you make them into idealised beings, not women, but gods, angels. What chance do they have, when you get back and you see them in the flesh, with their grey hair, their warts, their bulbous arms, their snide comments, their shrieking voices, their irritation with you and your painful hands, aching body, and your piles and your nightmares and your screaming.

Coughs, is in pain.

It's the girl I miss the most. Little Nancy. I know she wasn't my one, my blood, but I loved her as if she were. Her mother, Agnes, she, well I left my Lizzie for Agnes.

All those days and nights on the ice and you never once asked, never once bothered to find out, where did you come from, McLeod, McNish. Who are your people?

Did you used to play kick the can, when you were young? Wee heiders, leavo? What, wee heiders? That's heady football. What did you play as a boy? Heady football too? What did you call it? I liked wee heiders. I was the best in the street. Well at least in our tenement. Certainly amongst my brothers.

Jessie was my first. I was only twenty one when we married. We met at a church dance. That's where all the get-togethers took place. Where else will a boy meet a girl. I noticed her, she had long brown hair. Blue eyes. Curls, ringlets, well her mother made them go like that. But it didn't last and by the end of the evening, with all that dancing, her hair would fall out of all those grips and it would be straight again, with just a hint of a sweaty curl. Twenty and in love. You feel the world is made specially for you.

So many women died in childbirth. It wasn't unusual. But it was unusual for me. I lost my wife and my baby in one fell swoop. A widower at twenty four.

No, I didn't mourn for long. Why would I? I was young, had blood pounding through my veins, down my arteries, desperate to get my arms around a woman again. Ten months after being a widower I became a husband again. To Ellen. Fair Ellen. Sweet Ellen. Very curly hair, had Ellen. Tight curls that sprung back when you let them go. Very devout was Ellen. But we liked a drink together, my Ellen and me. Six years we lived together and then she died too.

Oh God, Lord, what are you doing to me? Are you testing me? What have you got against me? There's Robert, and George. You know what hard headed men they are. Bone idle, drink their money, beat their wives. Punish them, why don't you. Take their wives. Leave me my Ellen. Oh, God, how can you fight against such power. Such authority.

This time I waited three years. Thirty three when I married my third. Lizzie.

I should have had a score of children but I only had one. Only Thomas. One boy.

And Nancy. But she was never mine.

To sweethearts and wives, we toasted. I toasted both, my sweetheart and my wife.

You did too.

It wasn't only about tea. Anyone can bring tea. Ingratiate yourself by bringing tea, rise and shine. But you didn't sleep for seven days after we left the ice, after we couldn't stop at the ice, get off at night to pitch the tents, to sleep. Those seven days when we sailed to Elephant Island. You stayed awake. Only you. We all grabbed some sleep when we could, but not you, the eternal watch. The incessant vigil, Wild said.

And then we land on Elephant Island you'd think every man of them is roaring drunk! Gone off their heads. Land, hard, solid, real land beneath our feet. Not moving, not wet, not ice, God's earth. Some walk around aimlessly, some shiver as if they have palsy. Do you see how some fill their pockets with stones, Vincent, Holness, James, look how they roll along the beach, Bakewell, Kerr, pouring stones over their heads, Clark, Stevenson. We sleep a bit in our damp sleeping bags, then get up and join the others round the fire. Fire, a real fire made from branches, wood that we've collected. After sixteen months we have earth back beneath our feet.

Hudson has terrible boils and Blackborow's frost bite is so bad his toes are amputated.

There's lots to eat, no problem with food. Seals, Gentoo, ringed penguins, limpets. But no elephant seals, Boss, even though we're on elephant island.

Look, over there. What do you see? Can you see him? He's there. He's waiting. McLeod, Tom, come on my lad. Come here, come join us. It's the Boss with us. We're having a drink. Come, don't be shy. Look at you. I won't shake your hand. My hands are so painful, can't shake without yelping with pain, yelping like those dogs yelped knowing they were to be shot, but no, I won't think of that now, not with you here as well. Look Boss. It's McLeod. He's come to join us. Where's that whiskey. You'll have a wee dram, now, won't you.

Well, I have to say, it's good to see you, McLeod. It's doing me a power of good to see you.

What do you say to the Boss? He's looking good, isn't he. For a dead man, he's looking very good. Did you not know he died? Yes. He's a ghost now. Roaming the world, isn't that so, Boss.

What about you, McLeod. How's life treating you? What're you doing in Wellington?

Ah. You've come to see me. That is good. I'm very pleased to see you. I am. I am.

He suddenly catches a glimpse of something, someone further away and is horrified.

McLeod. Look over there. Can you see him? Can you, look, just behind that wall, over there. I swear I thought I saw… .Can you see him, Boss. Is it him? Is it, Lees? Oh no. I couldn't, I don't want, no, tell him to go, Boss. I don't want to see him, I couldn't cope, not here, not in my refuge. It's my place this. It's not for every riff raff, no gooder. Tell him to go. I won't have him here. I don't want to see him.

Do you think he heard? I can't see him anymore. Yes, of course it was him. I'd know him anywhere. He's even wearing that stupid hat he always wore, that fur hat, you know the one, no not fur, fur lined. Sticks up on the sides, folds over in the front. You know the one.

I won't have him here. This is my place. You're welcome Boss, but you're a ghost and you can come and go at will.

He hitched here, McLeod, on a boat. All the way from South Georgia. But he stopped in London first, to see his wife.

And you, McLeod. It does me good to see you. Have some Whiskey. Drink man, drink. I'll have some too, let's drink. It's good to see friends. Friends need a drink.

He drinks. He's in pain.

So how've you been, McLeod. I heard you got two Polar medals, silver and bronze. That is, wonderful. I'm proud of you, man. You're proud, aren't you, Boss. Yes. All proud. Silver and bronze.

No, I didn't get it, but that's alright. The Boss explained. Did you explain, Boss? Yes, I think he explained.

Were you scared, McLeod. Stuck on the boat, hearing that crack, that roar, that thunder, knowing there's no thunder only pressure, pushing, thrusting, pressing, stabbing at the hulk, at our, home.

We didn't know we'd get out. Now we can look back and we know we're safe. But we didn't know we'd be alright. Then. When we were listening, what was that, did you hear something. And every bang we heard we knew this could be the end, what would happen, this could be it, and then?

Did you see the light, McLeod? No. Only me then.

So how's your mother, McLeod? Dead? No! I'm sorry to hear that. Yes mine is too. And my father. And some of my brothers and sisters. I was the third eldest, of eleven. But you knew that. I told you. Have you forgotten? That's alright, McLeod. I forget lots of things too. We do, as we get older. Don't you find that?

Do you remember my Mrs Chippy? Of course you do. I know, she was a very special cat. But Shackleton shot my cat, you know. Yes of course you do.

There's a cat that comes to see me from time to time. It's a tabby, like Mrs Chippy. I'm not sure if it's a real Mrs, or a Mr, this one. Do you remember how she liked to tease those dogs, take a stroll across the roofs of the kennels, provoke them, but they were tethered, at a safe distance. She had such character, didn't she, McLeod. Do you remember how early on in the voyage she fell out the boat and it was only thanks to Hudson who heard her cries that he managed to stop the boat, go back and pick her up.

What? Who said that? Whose voice did I hear?

Green. It's Green's voice. Where are you Green? McLeod, did you hear, Green's here. He's come as well. Come lad, come let's see you. It's been a while. Not that long, mind you. I saw him only a few years ago. Did you know, McLeod? Did you, Boss? We met up. Come Green, come sit and we'll talk of how we met just a few years ago.

Yes, there he is, through the mist, look. He's coming. Green, come drink my lad. Come all of you, share with me. Let's get this bottle into us. I have another, tucked away, hidden in the boat where no-one can see. So we're alright. We've enough to spare.

He drinks.

Aye, I wish I had some provisions for you to cook up a feast for us now, Green. What a cook. The greatest chef on the planet. Isn't he? Isn't that so, McLeod, Boss. Yes. What concoctions he made. Imagine what he could do with fresh ingredients. Ah, a bit of seal liver, that's what I'd love now. Cooked on a blubber stove, black smoke pouring up, seal, penguin. Do you remember those young albatross we ate when we got to South Georgia, Boss. They tasted better than anything we could imagine. Flesh white and succulent, and bones not fully formed, soft, they melted in the mouth.

I said I'd tell you where we met. I was in hospital, well, thank you for your concern. I was told the cook from the

Endurance was in Wellington and was going to give a lecture. They allowed me out and Green saw me sitting in the audience. Come up, you said, didn't you Green. Look everyone there is a man who was actually there, who did the greatest open boat journey in the history of navigation. Come up lad, come on the stage. I don't want to tell a story of which I was not a part. But you were. Come tell these folk what really happened, the story of the boat journey from Elephant Island to South Georgia. And I go up and he says, look everyone, here in front of you is the one who made it possible because he was the one who caulked the boat with Marsten's painting oils and flour and seal blood, who fitted it and fixed it so that it had a chance against the waves and the seas and the currents and the, waves. It's thanks to him, this man here, that the James Caird was able to sail, that it did, that it got there, that it sailed. Without him, there would have been no story, no heroic adventure, just the tragedy that was the Endurance. Shackleton, none of them, without this man, would have, none, come back, returned, no-one...

They clap. They clap for me, that audience. Clap and clap and... it is so...

Hussey's playing the banjo, listen, and the penguins they're coming in to watch as he plays on deck. They always come particularly when he plays these good old Scots songs.

Sings 'Roamin' in the gloamin'.

They clap their flippers. They like real music. Hussey says, no, you're wrong, it's the Negro spirituals and a long way to Tipperary that keeps those penguins watching. But it's only the Scots music that makes them stay, flapping and clapping and laughing. Look, they'll break away and rush off in a panic if anything else is played.

Green, do you know that Shackleton shot my cat. Mrs Chippy was a he. But you know that.

Oh Lord, it's Lees. He's there again. I saw him there, I swear. He's standing and every time you look, he ducks behind the wall.

No Boss. You don't have any right to invite him in. This is my place. It's not up to you. No don't. No, I say. I don't want him here. Tell him to go.

Aghhhhh

He throws himself face down on his sleeping bag. He lies very still. He covers his eyes.

Has he gone?

He looks up, sees him and throws a can of soup at him.

Get away from here. You hear me. Get out.

I think he's gone.

McLeod. Can you see him? Has he gone? Are you sure?

He crawls out and grabs the bottle and drinks.

No, Jesus, he is here!

How did you get here! *(He starts boxing at him with fists.)* I told you to go. Get out of here!

Eventually he collapses on the ground.

I don't want him here.

Why doesn't he go if he knows he's not welcome. He won't go.

You sit there. Who're you smiling at? Wipe that nasty smile off... don't you smile at me.

Don't offer him my whiskey. It's mine. *(He grabs the bottle and drinks.)*

Useless

Arrogant

Waste of time

Waste of space

Made to clean the floors. Just like the rest of us. Couldn't cope, could you. Toff. Arrogant prig. Dobber. Nugget. Tumshie heid. You, with yer face like a bulldog chown a wasp.

Kept food for himself. Squirreled it. Took food from others, the fools, they wanted to exchange, wanted baccy, drink, grog. They were silly, didn't understand you need your own food, own rations.

On the boat, the skipper told him to row. But what did he do, lazy bastard, got into his sleeping bag. What do you say Boss. Should he get the polar medal for getting into his sleeping bag when the skipper said row.

Yes, of course he worked like a demon to bail out the boat, but then you would, wouldn't you, if you know you're going to sink.

I don't want to know what you've been doing. Shut your geggie!

I don't want to hear.

McLeod, talk to me, drown his voice. I don't want to know what he's been doing. Why he's in New Zealand. Isn't it far enough away? How far must I go? I can't go further, can't go anywhere, just here, on this wharf, that's as far as I can...

No Lees, don't speak to me. I don't have to explain myself to you.

It's bad fortune, that's what it is. Bad luck, I never had luck. My hands, my body, they're wracked with pain. That's not just an excuse! I worked until I was forced to stop. What happens when you can't work? You don't eat, you don't have a warm room and you don't have a proper bed. How can you understand. If it happened to you, would you end up sleeping in a boat on a wharf. Never. You'd be given help, mummy or daddy, aunty, uncle, friends, people from your class, they'll make sure you don't end up like this. They'll give you a job you can do, other jobs that don't need perfect hands, hands that work, money, they'll help you up, hand you what you need. Where are hands to help me? The only hands that help me are the dockers here, who don't have money themselves, but once a month they make a collection and give me some money, drink, food to survive. And they look away when they know I sleep in the lifeboat, make sure the tarpaulin is always there. We've got to look after Shackleton's Carpenter.

Don't mock me! I don't know why you got the polar medal, shirking in your sleeping bag, unwilling, unable to do anything. Yes, I didn't get it. I don't care, it's not important. McLeod, tell him it's not important. Is it important?

I don't want to be here. I want to be home. Where's home? I want my little Nancy. She would've cared for me, given me things, helped me when my hands curl up, freeze, die. She loved me, Uncle Harry, she called me. I wasn't the old carpenter to Nancy. Boss, do you think I should go back with you? Can you lift someone when you're a ghost? I don't mind lying there in Grytviken. Will there be enough space in that grave. Could you pick me up and fly me all the way. Perhaps it will happen in the blink of an eye.

There's such a noise now, Boss. What happened to that peace and quiet. I came for the peace and the quiet and all I hear is a rumble, a crashing. Those floes are pressing, Boss, they're crushing our ship. What do you say? Speak up. Shout! What is it? Am I going deaf? I can't hear you! All I hear is the ice rushing, gushing, pounding.

What? Where?

Oh my Lord, look over there. The light is coming. It's coming from the horizon. Can you see it? It's floating quickly directly from over there, look, you must be able to see. Don't tell me you can't see it. It's there, suspended, moving, it's coming so fast. Hold on, wait, it's not just one, no, no, there're lots of lights, they're coming all together. They're being carried by people, walking straight towards us. No floes, no ice, just walking straight towards us, here.

Boys! Hello!

Dr Macklin, Dr McIlroy!

Hudson, how's your boil, all gone now? Back to normal? That's good. Is there a scar?

Blackborow, you're older now, not a young twenty year old anymore. I see you're walking fine on those feet. Mr Wild... . What have you been doing? I heard you were in South Africa, serving beer to the Zulus. You always made gut rot. Did it get you too, in the end?How, and you've brought your ukulele. We'll have a song. Stephenson, Holness.

Bakewell, Rickinson, Kerr, still working on the ships. *(Salutes them.)*

Mr Wordie. My fellow Scot. I'm honoured. Mr Clark. Another Scot, but from Aberdeen. Well, you can't have everything, hey, Clarkie.

Vincent, you bully. You only looked out for one man, and that was always you. And Crean. You climbed the uncharted mountains of South Georgia, you and the Boss and the Skipper. And a fourth you all felt was there walking with you. You were brave and good. Mr Worsley. Even you've come. I don't know why you're here because you never liked me. No, that's alright. Water under the bridge. The greatest sea captain and navigator in the history of the world. Isn't that so? McLeod, Boss, isn't that so? Mr Hussey. Look Boss, he's brought his banjo. Oh we're going to sing tonight. How, you with your ukulele and Hussey, with your banjo, look we have an orchestra. And Mr Hurley is here and he's brought his cameras. He's going to capture this night, this special night, for prosperity.

This reunion of the boys from the Endurance. We're all together again. Come, let's go down into the ship, We're in our ship, sitting below deck, all cosy, all warm. Some grog and our pipes, music from the boys. Light engulfing us, enfolding us. Oh how we'll sing tonight!

Collapses.

Blackout.

The sound of gun salute.

TWO SISTERS

Two Sisters produced by New Vic Productions in association with Eastbourne Theatres, first performance 10 June 2010, first produced at Devonshire Park Theatre with the following cast:

EDITH Paola Dionisotti

RIKA Anita Dobson

Director Ninon Jerome

Producer Tony Milner, New Vic Productions

Lighting Gavin Davis

Production Manager Paul Debreczeny

Characters

EDITH, 75

RIKA, 71

EDITH and RIKA are sisters.

The play is set in 1996, on a kibbutz in northern Israel.

It is the morning after EDITH's 75th birthday party. There was a big celebration last night with most of the kibbutz attending. You wouldn't know EDITH was 75, apart from her incredibly lined face, though that's from years of being in the strong sun. She seems sprightly, loud, fit and well. RIKA on the other hand is far less energetic, whether this is as a result of life's woes or genuine illness is unsure. The play takes place on the last weekend of RIKA's two week holiday in Israel, where she has come to celebrate EDITH's birthday.

The play takes place in EDITH's small apartment on the kibbutz. The living room has a little kitchenette attached to it at one end and a bedroom off the other.

SCENE 1

EDITH is sitting in the lounge of her small apartment on the kibbutz. She is reading a book and drinking coffee. Her apartment is well furnished with many books lining the walls. She reads until RIKA eventually enters, obviously having just woken up.

EDITH: At long last! Good morning.

RIKA: Oy! Did I have a terrible night.

EDITH: You look as though you slept well enough.

RIKA: I hardly slept a wink.

EDITH: You look as though you slept.

RIKA: I'm telling you. Not a wink. The whole night.

EDITH: Now it's already not a wink. Before it was hardly a wink.

RIKA: Oy, will you stop giving me a hole in the head. Enough I didn't sleep. Now I have to listen to you hukking me.

EDITH: I only said you looked well.

RIKA: So, I look well but I feel terrible. What's better?

EDITH: You never slept well.

RIKA: When I was little it wasn't so bad.

EDITH: Never. Always problems.

RIKA: When I was little..

EDITH: I'm telling you. Never.

RIKA: You know better than me how I slept. You always know better even though it's me trying to sleep and not you.

EDITH: I've got a better memory.

RIKA: Ach, you also don't remember so well.

EDITH: Anyway. Coffee?

RIKA: Ahh, it won't kill me. One cup first thing in the morning.

(EDITH pours and serves the coffee, then sits and picks up her book again. She starts to read.)

RIKA: Nu, so you can't talk to me.

(She puts the book down.)

EDITH: So talk.

RIKA: The second last morning I'm here you have to read?

EDITH: So talk already.

RIKA: Who knows when we'll see each other again.

EDITH: You're coming back in a few months.

RIKA: Who knows!

EDITH: What do you mean, who knows? You're coming back. You said so.

RIKA: Who knows if I'll be alive in a few months.

EDITH: You'll be alive. How could you not be? With all those pills you take, you'll be alive.

RIKA: I don't take those pills for nothing, you know.

EDITH: I know.

RIKA: My doctor is very worried about me.

EDITH: Of course. He wouldn't be your doctor if he wasn't.

RIKA: And what's that supposed to mean?

EDITH: If your doctor said you were fine, you'd find someone else.

RIKA: I know my own body.

EDITH: You studied medicine?

RIKA: One doesn't always need to study to know.

EDITH: My sister the Professor.

RIKA: There are things I know.

EDITH: Nu.

RIKA: Nu, nu.

(Pause.)

RIKA: You had a good time last night.

EDITH: It was good, huh!

RIKA: So many people!

EDITH: Everybody turned out. They made so much effort.

RIKA: And so they should. One of the founding members turns seventy five. It's something.

EDITH: Yah! Seventy five. It's something, huh?

RIKA: It is. I'll be there in four years.

EDITH: Good. Now you've decided to survive a few more months. That's good.

RIKA: *(Laughing.)* If you can make seventy five, I'll bloody make seventy five.

EDITH: Since when have you become a swearer. You, the one who never swore.

RIKA: Bloody's not a swear word.

EDITH: It used to be for you.

RIKA: I've become coarse in my old age.

EDITH: Coarse! I'm the coarse one. You're the lady. The English lady.

RIKA: English lady! Who would have thought I'd end up looking like our grandmother!

EDITH: Not quite. You still manage to keep your knickers on.

RIKA: Oy, how they fell off in the middle of the street that time. I'll never forget..

EDITH: Were you actually there when it happened?

RIKA: No. Neither were you.

EDITH: Our grandmother!

RIKA: Mutti was so good with her. Just a mother-in-law. Not even her mother.

(Pause.)

They knew how to look after their old people in those days.

EDITH: Yah!

RIKA: It's such a shame Janine couldn't come to the party.

(Pause.)

I know she wanted to. But, you know kids. They intend to come, say they're going to come, you expect them, then, something happens, the boyfriend's this, the boyfriend's that…

EDITH: She could've come, Rika.

RIKA: Boyfriends are what's important at eighteen.

EDITH: Your great aunt doesn't turn seventy five every day.

RIKA: Her boyfriend threatened to leave her. What could she do? She wanted to come..

EDITH: She thinks of herself.

RIKA: Anyway, she'll be here today.

EDITH: Today's not the party.

RIKA: I am sorry, Edith.

EDITH: Ahh! She's still a lovely girl.

RIKA: She is, isn't she? She is wonderful. Something special.

EDITH: With this I have to agree. But..

RIKA: Headstrong. I know, she is. I worry.

EDITH: Now, there's something new.

RIKA: Why? I'm not such a worrier anymore.

EDITH: Rika! Are you kidding? If you didn't worry, I don't know what you'd do. What joy you'd get out of life.

RIKA: Honestly! As if I worry so much.

(EDITH shakes her head in disbelief.)

When? When do I worry?

I don't. I never worry. Mind you, I had reason to worry last night.

EDITH: What reason?

RIKA: You!

EDITH: What do you mean?

RIKA: You! The way you behaved.

EDITH: The way I behaved?

RIKA: Yes! The way you behaved!

EDITH: When? What did I do?

RIKA: You flirted!

EDITH: I flirted! You're mad!

RIKA: I'm telling you! You flirted like a young thing. A young thing Janine's age!

EDITH: With whom?

RIKA: With whom! As if you didn't know!

EDITH: Don't tell me you're talking about Natan!

RIKA: You know I am.

EDITH: And you call that flirting?

RIKA: I call that flirting!

EDITH: You don't know what flirting is. You should watch your grandchild, Janine. Now, that's flirting.

RIKA: She's eighteen. When an eighteen year old flirts it's cute.

EDITH: Cute!

RIKA: When a seventy five year old flirts, it's disgusting. Revolting.

EDITH: I wasn't flirting.

RIKA: So, sitting on his lap isn't flirting. At seventy five sitting on his lap! Drinking from his glass of whisky isn't flirting. Giggling isn't flirting.

EDITH: It wasn't whisky.

RIKA: Brandy! That makes it all alright?

EDITH: Stop being such a spoil sport.

RIKA: At your age it isn't a sport!

EDITH: It's always been a sport.

RIKA: Well it shouldn't be,

EDITH: What should I be doing, then?

RIKA: Knitting!

EDITH: I hate knitting.

RIKA: It's good for you!

EDITH: It's not.

RIKA: It keeps you supple.

EDITH: It gives you arthritis.

(Pause.)

RIKA: I'm worried about Janine. I think she's sleeping with that boy, that Ari.

EDITH: Of course she's sleeping with him.

RIKA: What do you mean, of course!

EDITH: Of course she is. What do you think they do together? Knit?

RIKA: She's so young.

EDITH: She's not so young. Eighteen isn't so young. Look what you were doing when you were eighteen.

RIKA: It was so different for us. In those days. Things were different.

EDITH: Plus ça change, plus ça la même chose.

RIKA: Now she's speaking French!

EDITH: I am a lady of culture, you see.

RIKA: I see a lady who flirts with a seventy five year old.

EDITH: Again with the flirting.

RIKA: I'm sorry. I was shocked. What can I do?

EDITH: You make Natan out to be a young bull. Meanwhile he can hardly stand, that poor old thing.

RIKA: He's a fool.

EDITH: You say fool, but I remember you dancing with him. Oy, could he dance!

RIKA: Fifty five years ago!

EDITH: *(Laughing.)* Yes. Fifty five years ago. He was a bull then, wasn't he, hey Rika? Remember?

RIKA: Yes, I remember. The schmendrick.

EDITH: He's not such a schmendrick.

RIKA: He was a schmendrick then and he's a bigger
schmendrick now.

EDITH: He's not such a fool.

(Pause.)

I know. Let's have some of that birthday cake.

RIKA: Ugh, I couldn't.

EDITH: Well I could.

(She brings out a very chocolatey looking cake. It is slightly past its sell-by date.)

Yum.

(She cuts a huge slice and starts to eat it, much to RIKA's disgust.)

What happened to your sweet tooth?

RIKA: You never used to like sweet things.

EDITH: But you! All the time. That's all you ate, sweets.
Nougat. Marzipan. Chocolate. Only if it's sweet.

RIKA: We all grow up. You've got to look after yourself, your
health.

EDITH: Papa used to buy you sweets all the time.

RIKA: Don't exaggerate.

EDITH: All the time. He was always bringing nougat home for
you.

RIKA: Honestly!

EDITH: Of course he did. Nougat for his little precious.

RIKA: For his little precious! You were just as precious.

EDITH: Of course I wasn't. You were the precious. I was the
fighter.

RIKA: What fighter?

EDITH: All those fights I was constantly having with them.

RIKA: What fights?

EDITH: About coming to Palestine.

RIKA: Mutti and Papa were only too pleased that you were going.

EDITH: Rika. You have such a selective memory. There were terrible arguments.

RIKA: No there weren't.

EDITH: Kristallnacht hadn't happened yet.

RIKA: Oh yes. That's true.

EDITH: Kristallnacht was November 38, remember. I left in April 38.

RIKA: I don't remember fights. Anyway, you went with friends, with a group. I was alone. *(Pause.)* The story of my life.

EDITH: Rika. Please.

RIKA: I was alone. What can I do? I was alone.

(Pause.)

EDITH: This cake is good.

RIKA: Make yourself sick. What do I care?

(Pause.)

EDITH: I'm sorry you were alone. You were young, Rika. You couldn't've come with us.

RIKA: Who says I could've. Am I saying that? Am I saying I should've come with you? Am I?

EDITH: Besides, we were all Zionists. Socialists. You didn't care. You were never interested.

RIKA: I was young.

EDITH: You never cared.

RIKA: Nu.

EDITH: We went as a group. We planned it for over a year.

RIKA: I know. It was a group.

EDITH: You were so uninterested. We were all so much older as well. Four years older.

RIKA: Three.

EDITH: Mostly four.

RIKA: No it was three.

EDITH: Three, four. What does it matter now? What's a year?

RIKA: A year now is nothing. A year when you're fourteen is something.

EDITH: That's true. Alright. Three. Nu. There you have it. There, you've won. Are you happy now? It was three. Mazel tov. Three.

RIKA: Oh stop it! Honestly. I'm sick and tired of the way you do that.

EDITH: Do what?

RIKA: That. When you know I'm right and you make a big song and dance, so that, even though I'm right, I'm now wrong. You should have been a politician.

EDITH: <u>You </u>should have been a politician.

RIKA: Me? I'm too honest. I can't tell a lie. If you paid me, I couldn't lie. But you….

EDITH: Are you bad, if you lie? Are you a bad person, do you think, if you lie? I can lie so easily. I don't even notice it.

RIKA: You're terrible, Edith. Even little things you lie.

EDITH: I know. I started thinking about that recently. Ach! But you know what I decided? They're only white lies. I've never harmed anybody with it.

RIKA: Harm? Well, that depends, doesn't it.

EDITH: Nobody's ever died because I lied.

RIKA: Alright. That's the extreme of harm. There's more to harm than dying.

EDITH: More than dying?

RIKA: You know what I mean. I mean, other things. There's other things that you can do, that you have done. Things that harm, yet you'd walk away and not even realised anything had happened.

EDITH: Ach, nonsense.

RIKA: I'm telling you, Edith. You don't realise…

EDITH: Listen, what did you think when Natan sang last night?

RIKA: What did I think? I think you're changing the subject. That's what I think. I think you don't want to hear when I'm telling you the truth.

EDITH: Rika. I'm seventy five. Do I want to hear now how I'm not a perfect being? You know what? I know it already!

RIKA: But you can do something …

EDITH: I'm not going to do anything about it. I'm too old. Life will continue exactly the same if I change or if I don't. Go on. Tell me what you thought when Natan started singing.

RIKA: I thought what a wonderful voice!

EDITH: No. Tell me the truth.

RIKA: I thought, what an idiot. He still thinks he's the greatest.

EDITH: *(Laughing.)* Yes.

RIKA: But he's really a fool.

EDITH: That too.

RIKA: I don't know what you see in him, Edith. After Joseph..

EDITH: Joseph's dead, Rika.

RIKA: But he was so..

EDITH: He's dead. Natan's alive. He's around. He's a real person.

RIKA: Joseph was so…

EDITH: He was so, but now he is so dead.

RIKA: You can't just forget him.

EDITH: He's not here anymore. He doesn't sit with me at night. I can't talk to him about the film on the television, about the concert on the radio. He doesn't advise me anymore on which book to read. He just isn't there. What's the point of sitting round remembering him. I want to carry on living. Not sit on his smouldering pyre. I was never prepared to spend the rest of my life living with a ghost.

RIKA: You can't just forget.

EDITH: I'm not going to identify myself as a widow. I am not Edith, the widow. I am Edith, a woman.

RIKA: Old woman.

EDITH: Old, but alive.

RIKA: And me? You think I'm not alive?

EDITH: You're alive. You just like to live in a cave.

RIKA: It's safe in a cave. The light's not so bright, and you know where the walls are.

EDITH: But there are bats in caves.

RIKA: The bats are my memories.

EDITH: They fester, and mould, and infect the air in the cave.

RIKA: I need my memories. I'm not you. I can't forget. Not care.

EDITH: It's not a case of not caring. Do you really think I don't care?

RIKA: I think you won't care.

EDITH: I do care.

RIKA: Caring. It affects my life, this caring. It's too much. I see someone, a beggar, a homeless, those people, with their blankets, their dogs. They sit with their badly written signs on scraps of cardboard. Hungry. I don't want to see it. I don't want to feel it.

EDITH: So you don't give them anything?

RIKA: I feel. It's enough.

(Pause.)

Edith?

EDITH: Yes.

RIKA: Sometimes, I … Oh, it's so ridiculous. Grown woman. Old woman.

EDITH: What?

RIKA: You'll laugh. You'll mock me.

EDITH: No, I won't. Go on. Tell me.

RIKA: It's so ridiculous, but, things like that.

EDITH: Like what?

RIKA: Like, giving money to beggars, or not giving money, and other things, like your white lies, things that … when you're not really sure what's right, and what's wrong, things on the … what's that bloody word, they talk about it with the stars…you know, when things are not one thing or another…

EDITH: On the cusp? Is that what you mean?

RIKA: Yes! Cusp! That's the word. Things that are on the cusp. Not right, not wrong.

EDITH: I'm still here with you, Rika.

RIKA: I want my mother. I want to speak to her and ask her what's right. And what's wrong. And Papa too. I want them to tell me what to think.

(Pause.)

Does that seem very pathetic, Edith?

EDITH: Pathetic? You were so young when you got out, Rika.

RIKA: I know.

EDITH: I think of them too.

RIKA: Do you, Edith?

EDITH: Of course I do. You think I can't care, but I can and I do. I think of those two people who were so good. Good people.

RIKA: Never a swear word, never a loud word…

EDITH: Decent. Good people. Just good, solid people.

RIKA: Oy, I tell you Edith.

EDITH: Don't tell me, I know.

RIKA: I'm telling you. Not a day goes by. Do you know that?

EDITH: You don't have to tell me. I know.

RIKA: Not a day.

(She sighs. Pause.)

EDITH: How didn't we know?

RIKA: I ask myself that.

EDITH: How could we not have known!

RIKA: I don't know.

EDITH: We didn't. Did we, Rika? Was there something there that told us and we just pushed it away? Why would we push it? Did we just ignore it? *(Sighs.)* That selfishness of youth.

RIKA: Difficult times.

EDITH: Yah, difficult, sure, but, you know what I mean, don't you? When you know something, it's there inside you and you know it but, you don't necessarily recognise it. You don't, *know* it, know it.

RIKA: At the end we were *told* they were alright. Did you suspect, even a flicker of a doubt …

EDITH: No.

RIKA: I always felt one day mutti and papa would come for us. I knew it in the depths of my being. They would come. We would be together. A family again. *(Pause.)* And then he phoned, that man

EDITH: *(Exaggeratedly ironic.)* They're in America, yes, absolutely sure, completely certain. In America.

RIKA: They're fine, in America, fine.

(Pause.)

We were so…

EDITH: when we found out … the truth…

(Pause.)

RIKA: So, you see. You know it. But the truth is, you're wrong.

EDITH: Yes.

RIKA: Somebody tells you it's white, you believe him. But that doesn't make it white. Not when it is really black.

(Pause.)

Oi, enough already. Let's watch some telly. Put on the telly, Edith. Let's have some biscuits. Some telly and biscuits. And tea. Those nice biscuits. The ones you keep for good. Not those Israeli ones, the other ones. Those good ones.

EDITH: But they're the special ones.

RIKA: So? The special ones you can't use on your sister? How many sisters have you got? One sister! The only sister you have and you can't give her a decent biscuit.

(EDITH goes to the cupboard to get the biscuits. She opens them and is horrified.)

EDITH: My God, Rika. Have you been at these?

RIKA: Honestly! The treasure of Tutenkamen!

EDITH: Tutenkamen!

RIKA: You'd think I'd raided the tomb. Just a biscuit.

EDITH: Just ten more like.

RIKA: Ten! Anyway, I don't know why you buy a box of biscuits that has so few in it. You buy biscuits for mice. A mouse would be satisfied from one biscuit. Am I a mouse?

EDITH: So why didn't you eat the Israeli ones. They're big enough for elephants.

RIKA: Put the television on already. Enough with the animals.

(EDITH puts on the television. Tanks are rolling into Lebanon. A woman wails and moans in Arabic.)

EDITH: Oh my God!

RIKA: Oh God!

EDITH: How is it possible?

RIKA: How could it be?

EDITH: We have brutalised our boys.

RIKA: That poor woman.

EDITH: A socialist state, born out of brutality, and now, us?

RIKA: What she must be going through.

EDITH: I think of scenes from the Warsaw ghetto when I see this.

RIKA: You can't compare.

EDITH: I wish we can't.

RIKA: Of course you can't. These people start it. Look how they throw the stones. They must protect themselves.

EDITH: Stones? And bombs?

RIKA: Oy, Edith, do me a favour. Switch it off. I can't stand it. Honestly, I just can't cope with all those problems. Enough I've got my own problems. Enough I see beggars in the streets.

(EITH turns it off and goes to make the tea.)

Janine should be here about five, huh? She said five, didn't she? I'm so looking forward to seeing her. I hope that Ari doesn't come with her. I'm so pleased she's going off to university. And so close to me. It's wonderful isn't it Edith? Eighteen. Her whole life ahead of her. What an opportunity. She can do anything she wants with her life. Imagine.

(Pause. EDITH returns with the tea.).)

When we were eighteen… you were married already, working the fields like a donkey, like a horse. And me, I was …agh! But Janine, for her, it's so, exciting.

(Pause.)

He is awful, isn't he, Edith? That Ari.I mean it's not just me who thinks that, is it? What do you think?

EDITH: Ach, he's alright. He's a kid.

RIKA: There's kids and there's kids.

EDITH: Ach, he's… he's fine. What is he, a bit of a shvitzer, a show-off.

RIKA: What does she see in him? They argue all the time. He threatens to go off with others, messes her about. She gets upset. Cries every five minutes. And besides, he's, so…

EDITH: So what?

RIKA: So, dark.

EDITH: So dark? What's that supposed to mean?

RIKA: I mean, all that rubble round his chin..

EDITH: Rubble?

RIKA: Rubble, not rubble, you know, ach man, what's it called?

EDITH: Stubble?

RIKA: Stubble. You see. I told you. It's happening all the time.

EDITH: It's only a word, Rika.

RIKA: Yes, only a word, but, that's the beginning. Isn't it? A word here, a word there. Earlier. Now again.

EDITH: It's only a word.

RIKA: It's the beginning, isn't it?

EDITH: Don't exaggerate.

RIKA: God, Edith. These things are genetic.

EDITH: Mutti and Papa weren't..

RIKA: Well we don't know, do we. They could've been, if they'd…

EDITH: There weren't any signs.

RIKA: They were too young. They wouldn't have then, anyway, shown signs I mean.

EDITH: It was only our grandmother.

RIKA: Yes. Oh God, Edith.

EDITH: I tell you what. I'll buy you knickers with strong elastic.

(RIKA looks shocked for a minute, then they both laugh.)

RIKA: Some joke!

EDITH: As long as you can laugh about it.

RIKA: But for how long?

EDITH: You know what I think Rika. Listen to me, I'm telling you. If it happens, then you won't know what's happened to you. Will you? If it doesn't, then there's no point in worrying about it now. Is there?

RIKA: There's only one problem with your logic.

EDITH: What?

RIKA: It doesn't take two seconds to happen. It's gradual. You see it coming. Imagine that, sitting in your cave, getting crazier and crazier. Those bats all about you until you become a bat yourself.

EDITH: Listen, Rika. You haven't got Alzheimer's.

RIKA: How do you know?

EDITH: You're too old! You would've had it by now.

RIKA: That's not true.

EDITH: Well then, all I can say is, worry. Spend the rest of your life worrying in case you get it.

RIKA: Why shouldn't I worry? What else have I got to do?

EDITH: Worry about this country – the bombs, the killing.

RIKA: I should worry about people I don't know? Pictures on television?

EDITH: You don't care, Rika. That's your problem. You've never cared for others. I care for all the people around me. For my community, my kibbutz. I am a Socialist.

RIKA: Socialism! Smocialism. What's so great about that! It's all about privatisation now anyway.

EDITH: No it's not!

RIKA: You think the kibbutz cares for you? Only your family cares, Edith. Me, your sister. And a few, good friends. But most of your friends are dead or dying when you're seventy five.

EDITH: If we didn't care for each other, for the community, for mankind, what's the point? If you want your life to mean something.

RIKA: Your life has meant something. To you. You enjoyed it.

EDITH: Enjoy!

RIKA: Yes. Don't dismiss it. To be able to say, I enjoyed my life. What else does one want? Huh?

EDITH: But everything's changed. I want my kibbutz as it was.

RIKA: Well nobody else does.

EDITH: Natan does.

RIKA: That fool.

EDITH: The old ones.

RIKA: They don't count anymore. You don't count anymore.

(Pause.)

EDITH: When do you stop counting?

RIKA: When nobody asks you.

EDITH: Asks you?

RIKA: Nobody asks your opinion. Nobody asks your advice. Nobody asks you out. Nobody is interested. Only can you still look after yourself. Do you wee on the floor. Do you poo in the bidet. Do we need to put you in a home yet?

EDITH: Jesus you can be bloody depressing, Rika.

RIKA: C'est la vie.

EDITH: C'est doesn't have to be la vie.

RIKA: It is la bloody vie, whether you like it or not.

EDITH: It's not like that for me.

RIKA: It will be.

EDITH: It doesn't have to be.

RIKA: Why should things be so different for you?

EDITH: I'm not you. I never have been. My life is good.

RIKA: Well at least you've got over that earlier crap.

EDITH: Crap, Rika? Is this you speaking?

RIKA: Yes, crap. I want to say crap. I've spent my life not saying it and now I'm going to make up for lost time. Crap, crap, crap.

EDITH: That's the worst you can say?

RIKA: Nu. I'm starting slowly.

(EDITH laughs.)

RIKA: I'm going to have a little lie-down before Janine comes. Do you know Edith, the truth is, if it wasn't for Janine, I would feel a lot worse. She makes me feel needed. You've got to be needed in life, otherwise…

EDITH: Rika…

RIKA: What?

EDITH: Nothing. Have a lie-down. It'll do you good.

Blackout

SCENE 2

It is later on that same day, around five in the afternoon. RIKA is pacing the room, looking out of the window from time to time to see if Janine is coming. EDITH is on the phone

EDITH: I wish you'd stop looking all the time.

(RIKA sits down and picks up some newspaper too.)

RIKA: Pass me your glasses.

EDITH: Why don't you get your own?

RIKA: So, don't.

EDITH: *(Passing her the glasses.)* I can't believe how lazy you are.

RIKA: Fuss, fuss.

EDITH: I'm not fussing. I just can't believe how lazy you are.

RIKA: I'm not. I worked all my life.

EDITH: Worked!

RIKA: Yes, worked. I had my job. And I brought up my daughter, <u>and</u> my grand-daughter.

EDITH: Worked in that agency.

RIKA: What's wrong with 'that agency'?

EDITH: Well if that's what you call work.

RIKA: What would you call it then?

EDITH: Sitting around gossiping.

RIKA: Just because I got on well with the girls who worked there. Would you prefer me to have been miserable?

EDITH: No, of course not.

(Pause.)

I know you miss your work, Rika. I know it's not much fun now.

RIKA: I'm absolutely fine, thank you.

EDITH: I worry about you.

RIKA: You never worry about anyone.

EDITH: I do, honestly. I do worry about you.

RIKA: Really? So, go on, nu. When you say, worry, what do you actually mean?

EDITH: I think about you.

RIKA: That's not worry.

EDITH: I think about you a lot.

RIKA: That's worry? You haven't got a clue. Worry is when you get palpitations and you get hot round the back of your neck when you can't sit and the whole night passes and you haven't slept a wink because the same horrible thought goes round and round your head, and you put on the radio but don't hear a word because the thought, the image doesn't leave you. That's worry.

EDITH: Well I think, and then I think some more. And I start wondering what you are actually doing. Right then. Then I think of you in your little flat, sitting in the chair, with a book in your lap. And the book's been there for a while. And you are looking at nothing. And you've been sitting looking at nothing for most of the morning. And the phone hasn't rung. And no-one's knocked at the door. And you forget to eat. And you don't drink. And eventually you get up and find your eyes are wet.

RIKA: It's my fault you have an imagination?

EDITH: So, I'm wrong?

RIKA: Of course you're wrong.

EDITH: So what do you do every day?

RIKA: This and that. Different things. Read, watch telly, play bridge.

EDITH: I thought that's fallen through.

RIKA: I play cards. Solitaire. Things like that.

EDITH: Solitaire?

RIKA: I go out, do things. Go shopping, go to the cinema. And Janine … I told you, I don't know what I'd do without that girl.

EDITH: More than can be said of that daughter of yours.

RIKA: She's busy.

EDITH: She's busy! All her life, Laura She's-busy Abrahams has been busy. Ballet, tennis, elocution, friends, exams. Busy, busy, busy. And now, well, what's news, busy! That woman..

RIKA: Oh leave her for goodness sake. I don't need her. She's fine. If I needed her, she'd be there for me. Thank God I don't need her. I can manage fine on my own.

EDITH: I do worry you know.

RIKA: Listen. Worry about yourself. Do me a favour.

EDITH: Oishh, you! You're such a …

RIKA: A nothing. I'm such a nothing.

EDITH: Now you really sound ridiculous. I'm such a nothing. For goodness sake. Do you really believe that? Because if you do, I'd be seriously worried.

RIKA: Hoh! Back to the worried.

(Pause. She looks out the window again.)

I tell you though, I am worried now..

EDITH: You see five minutes can't go by without you worrying.

RIKA: No, but, where is she?

(Pause.)

I can't understand it. She should've been here by now.

(Pause.)

I mean, even if she'd left late, like, ten say, which she said she wouldn't , she said she'd leave straight after breakfast, but even if she had, she would've been here by now.

(Pause.)

Is there a reason you're so calm, Edith?

EDITH: Not everyone worries like you, Rika.

RIKA: Something's happened.

EDITH: Nothing's happened.

RIKA: How can you be so sure? Oh, my God. I know it. Something's happened to her. I can feel it in my bones.

EDITH: Nothing's happened!

RIKA: How can you be so sure? Something's happened to her! I know it.

EDITH: Will you stop it already. I'm telling you. Nothing's happened.

RIKA: But how can you be sure? What do you know? You do know, you know something, don't you? Tell me. What is it?

(Pause.)

Tell me!

EDITH: She's not coming.

RIKA: What?

EDITH: I'm sorry, Rika. She was supposed to phone you by now. To tell you. I wasn't supposed to have to tell you. It wasn't up to me.

RIKA: But when did she tell you?

EDITH: Yesterday, before the party. She phoned. That's why I was annoyed with her.

RIKA: Why isn't she coming?

EDITH: She was supposed to phone.

RIKA: She is going to meet me at the airport tomorrow though, isn't she? She wants more time with that Ari? Is that it?

EDITH: She's not going back. To England. With you.

RIKA: What? That's impossible. What about…university.

EDITH: She's not going. She'll write to them. She's her own boss.

RIKA: But … university.

(Pause.)

You! You put her up to this. I knew it.

EDITH: Me? What Rubbish you talk.

RIKA: It has the.. the..what's that damned word, the.. hallmarks of you, all over it. Everything, everything I've ever wanted in life, you've managed to spoil. Everything! Everything has always gone your way. I've been the one to lose out, to miss the opportunity, to be forgotten about. now the one person… the one person…. Just the same….. always …everyone…

EDITH: Everyone what?

RIKA: Always went with you. They always did what you wanted. Now you've got Janine and I go home with no-one.

EDITH: I haven't got Janine, Rika. She's not at this kibbutz.

RIKA: But she's here in Israel. Why's she staying here? Did she say? Did she give me a message?

EDITH: She was upset. She said she couldn't speak to you because, you'd be too upset.

RIKA: But she still could've … spoken to me..

EDITH: She didn't want to. She said she'd phone tomorrow.. today that means, after lunch. She should've phoned. I shouldn't be expected to have to…

RIKA: Cope with a pathetic old woman.

EDITH: Not pathetic, Rika. I can understand..

RIKA: No you can't. You've never been able to understand me.. because … you've never tried. You bully you. You always bullied me. You're a bully.

EDITH: Me bully?

RIKA: Yes. You always..

EDITH: I can't believe you can say that. It's not true.

RIKA: It's true. It's so true.

EDITH: No. You're the one. You always got everything you wanted.

RIKA: I've never had anything.

EDITH: You've had everything!

RIKA: No. Nothing. What have I had?

EDITH: Beauty. You had beauty.

RIKA: Beauty? What good is beauty?

EDITH: You were always beautiful.

RIKA: What good did it do me?

EDITH: Everyone always chased you, loved you.

RIKA: No. They loved you.

EDITH: They laughed with me. You they loved.

RIKA: Beauty!

EDITH: Yes. Beauty. You were always so beautiful. Even now, you're beautiful. Look at me with my lines, my crags.

RIKA: They laughed with you.

EDITH: Everyone always adored you.

RIKA: Do you really think I'm beautiful?

EDITH: Yes. I always have. And hated you for it.

RIKA: *(Smiling a bit.)* Really? That's nice.

The telephone rings

RIKA: Oh my God. It must be Janine. You answer it, Edith. Tell her, I'm too upset to talk.

EDITH: Nonsense. Of course you must talk to her. Hear her explanation. *(She picks up the phone.)* Hello. Hello Janine. Yes, I have. … She'll tell you. … Here she is.

(RIKA furiously indicates she won't come to the phone. EDITH continues to beckon her to come.)

She's… just coming now, Janine. Hold on a moment…

(Covering the mouthpiece.)

Will you come already?

(RIKA grabs the phone, stifling sobs.)

RIKA: Hello, who is it?... Oh, hello Janinie.... I'm alright, thank you..... Yes, I am..... Fine... She told me.... I understand...Yes, it's your choice....Of course.... I'm alright... Oh my God, Janinie, how could you? How could you? Oh my God,..

(EDITH takes the phone and RIKA collapses in the chair.)

EDITH: Hello. Hello Janine. Yes. Not too good. As you see. .... No that doesn't mean you have to go back. *(RIKA pricks up her ears at this.)* Of course you shouldn't. *(RIKA glares furiously at her.)* That means, you could if that's want you really want to do. *(EDITH moves away with the phone. RIKA is crying gently and goes off to find a tissue.)* Don't do anything rash. Just, leave the decisions. We'll speak tomorrow. Think about it until then. Then decide. You've got to live for yourself, not your grandmother. She'll get over it. ... Israel is a country that needs young people. And Ari, that sweet boy. You need time together to work things out. I really think you should stay..... We'll speak tomorrow, sweetheart. *Ciao. (She puts down the phone as RIKA comes back in wiping her eyes.)*

RIKA: I'm only thinking of her, what's good for her.

EDITH: Of course you are. Poor Janine. What she's going through now.

(RIKA doesn't respond.)

I can just imagine it. Sorry Ari. We might've had a future together but now we'll never know because my grandmother needs me to go home with her. Because she can't be by herself.

RIKA: She's a child. She needs family. Support. Love.

EDITH: She has love. She has Ari.

RIKA: That's not the sort of love you need. That's alright as an add-on, but you need the other kind of love. Unconditional love, the one that only a parent or grandparent can give. That Ari. He just makes her cry.

EDITH: That's what it's about when you're young and working out what it's all about. It's only later that we stop the crying and talking and working things out.

RIKA: I never stopped the crying.

EDITH: Why do you always bring it back to you?

RIKA: I'm not.

EDITH: We were talking about Janine. About how she needs to work things out for herself.

RIKA: It's hard to work things out for yourself when you're eighteen. You end up doing things, not even making decisions, just doing things, going in one direction rather than another. It's random. Then you suffer the consequences, and all your life you cry.

EDITH: You didn't spend your life crying, Rika.

RIKA: I hid the crying but I never stopped it. Your image of me? The one in the chair. That's been true all my life.

EDITH: Oh rubbish! You just talk pure rubbish. Crap. Shit.

RIKA: See, you don't understand.

EDITH: Rika. I'm seventy five. You're seventy one. Granted we don't live in each other's pockets. But, all these years we've written to each other, phoned each other at least once a month and these days it's about once a week. Plus, every single year I've seen you for at least a week, if not two or even three. Now please, don't tell me that I've missed out something so big, in my sister's life.

RIKA: What did you want me to do? Write you every time I cried? Phone up every time I felt terrible. Come rushing to my big sister? What good would it have done? You never were there for me. Ever. Even when we were little..

EDITH: You didn't need me then.

RIKA: No, not then. I had my mother and my father. But I did need you when I first came to Israel. That fourteen year old needed a bit of help, guidance, love. She didn't know her arse from her elbow. Excuse my French. Or don't. I've forgotten that I swear now.

EDITH: How old was I for God's sake? I wasn't old enough to be a surrogate mother. I was eighteen. We all missed our parents. You had our aunt. She looked after you.

RIKA: I wanted to be close to you.

EDITH: I didn't have time for it.

RIKA: You didn't have time for me. You were very cruel.

EDITH: I was not! When was I cruel?

RIKA: There are so many occasions.

EDITH: Name me one.

RIKA: Do we really want to rake this all up?

EDITH: Yes. I don't think I'm cruel. I don't think I can be cruel. So I need you to tell me when.

RIKA: Alright. I will. One example. Do you remember the first time I came to the kibbutz.

EDITH: Yes. I remember. We had fun. We danced in the dining room. You danced all night. How cruel was that?

RIKA: Not all night, because you all had to be up at four to work in the fields before it got too hot.

EDITH: Of course we did. It was summer. We all got up to start work at four.

RIKA: Yes. And I had to as well. You said I had to. If I was staying in the kibbutz and eating the kibbutz food, I had to work for it.

EDITH: Quite right. I still think so. Life was hard. We all had to work.

RIKA: I was fifteen, for Christ's sake.

EDITH: Old enough to work.

RIKA: Yes, old enough to work.

EDITH: You should have woken up.

RIKA: So you remember the occasion?

EDITH: I remember that you showed up at eight, just in time for breakfast. .

RIKA: Yes. Terrible crime. To miss work on the first day.

EDITH: It was in those days.

RIKA: Nobody else said a thing. Everyone was friendly and happy and gathered round me chatting and laughing. But you. You were the one who had to shout in the dining room about who did I think I was. Why did I think I was special. Time to stop being Papa's little princess.

EDITH: They were all round you again, you see. Bees round the honey pot.

RIKA: It was so embarrassing. I didn't know where to look. What to say.

EDITH: I just wanted you to know… that's all.. just to know that you couldn't ….

RIKA I knew I wasn't part of the group. That I'd never be part of your group.

EDITH: That you couldn't do whatever you wanted. And it would be alright. They were all my friends. For goodness' sake, Rika. What did you expect of me? We were building a state, a nation. A hoe in one hand, a gun in the other…… Arabs fighting us. You were just another burden.

RIKA: I know.

EDITH: I don't mean… burden, but, at the time…

RIKA: Well, it's all in the past now

EDITH: God it is. What are we on about as though it was yesterday. We're talking over fifty years ago, fifty seven years ago, for God's sake.

RIKA: I know. *(getting up.)* I've got to go to the lav.

EDITH: Go. Have you been today?

RIKA: No. I'll go sit a bit. See if anything happens.

EDITH: Yes. You do that. I'll.. I'll wait for you. Then we can sort out supper. We can go to the communal dining room for supper tonight instead of eating here. Shall we? We'll see who we'll see there. Maybe, it'll be fun. We can still have fun. We're not too old to have fun. Are we? Are we?

(RIKA exits.)

Blackout

SCENE 3

RIKA and EDITH are getting ready for bed. It is around ten o'clock at night.

EDITH: I'm glad you agreed to go to the dining room.

RIKA: Think of it as another birthday present.

EDITH: What nother? Where's the first?

RIKA: Me. I'm the first. Here with you.

EDITH: That's a present? Alright, I'm only joking. It's a wonderful present. The best! Thank you my little sister!

RIKA: Nu.

EDITH: I love you being here.

RIKA: You don't. We spend our time fighting.

EDITH: I love a fight. What can I tell you!

RIKA: You love a fight? I hate it!

EDITH: You hate it? But you do it so well!

RIKA: I always lose!

EDITH: Never!

RIKA: Always! Anyway. Sleep well. My last night here. Oy!

EDITH: Yah! You sleep well.

RIKA: I won't, of course.

EDITH: Try!

(The phone suddenly rings.)

RIKA: My God, who can that be? God, it must be Janine. Something's happened..

EDITH: *(Picking up the phone.)* Hello? … Ahh, it's you….

What's up?….. Did you?

RIKA: Who is it?

EDITH: Really? ….That is so crazy….

RIKA: Who is it?

EDITH: Nobody.

RIKA: Nobody?

EDITH: Just a minute…. *(To RIKA.)* It's only Natan. Go to bed.

RIKA: At this time he phones?

EDITH: Just Rika….. Natan says goodbye if he doesn't see you before you go…

RIKA sits down and listens to the conversation

Why don't you go to bed?…. No, Rika. She's sitting here, like some…no, it's ok…..

RIKA gets up and leaves the room. EDITH speaks more quietly

Oh you are silly….. nonsense…. Why on earth would we want to? At my age! At your age! We've known each other for ever. You're looking for a nurse…. I was never….. no, find someone younger…. You are an idiot. ….She'd be horrified, horrified.

RIKA comes back into the room

Anyway, I must go. Speak to you later.

RIKA: Who would be horrified?

EDITH: No-one.

RIKA: What are you plotting?

EDITH: Plotting? How ridiculous.

RIKA: Plotting? How ridiculous. That's exactly what you say whenever you're up to something. 'Plotting, how ridiculous'. This is so déjà vu!

EDITH: Well, you haven't deja vued this before – I can promise you.

RIKA: So what is it?

EDITH: Can you imagine, the fool wants to move in with me. What do you think?

RIKA: What do I think?

EDITH: Absurd, huh?

RIKA: Absurd isn't the word for it.

EDITH: What is then?

RIKA: It's utterly ridiculous.

EDITH: Is utterly ridiculous more than absurd?

RIKA: Grow up, Edith!

EDITH: Oh alright, I'll stop. But …

RIKA: But what?

EDITH: I must admit there is something quite appealing…

RIKA: What's appealing about that old fart…

EDITH: Old fart, Rika!

RIKA: Yes, bloody old fart, moving in with you. Using your things, taking over your things. How could you bear it?

EDITH: Well, there are some appealing things.

RIKA: Like what, for example?

EDITH: It gets lonely.

RIKA: What gets lonely? You're never alone. You have people around you all the time, for God's sake. Lonely! I can't believe you.

EDITH: At night, sometimes.

RIKA: At night?

EDITH: Yes.

RIKA: What do you mean, at night.

EDITH: Well, you know….what happens at night?

RIKA: You go to sleep.

EDITH: Yes, but that's not all there is to the night. Or, all there needs be..

RIKA: You watch television. *(Pause.)* Edith, don't tell me you're talking about… sex. Are you?

EDITH: Sex?

RIKA: Yes. Are you, Edith?

EDITH: I might be.

RIKA: Are you still interested in sex?

EDITH: I don't know.

RIKA: What do you mean you don't know. It's your body. You can tell if you, you know…

EDITH: It takes two to tango.

RIKA: But you'd know if you, fancied it.

EDITH: Well I don't fancy it, just by myself. I might if someone else was around…

RIKA: You know what? I don't want this, I am not having a conversation with my seventy five year old sister about her having sex, especially at this time of night. It's not for me.

EDITH: Do you think I'm being silly, Rika?

RIKA: You could say that.

EDITH: Don't you ever … you know…

RIKA: No. I don't. If there's one thing I am absolutely sure about, it's that.

EDITH: You were never, really, not really..

RIKA: How would you know?

EDITH: Well, I suppose I don't, but you would've …said something. Spoken about it. Something.

RIKA: You don't know me at all! Not at all!

EDITH: So, tell me. Were you interested? When you were younger?

RIKA: So are you seriously thinking of letting him move in?

EDITH: You ignored my question.

RIKA: You ignored mine.

EDITH: Yes. I am. Now answer mine.

RIKA: Of course I won't answer yours. It's my own business. It has nothing to do with you. Whatsoever.

EDITH: It's been a long time since Paul died. But, you had a good relationship..

RIKA: I don't want to talk about it.

EDITH: You did, though. I know you did. Maybe I just want to believe you did.

RIKA: I did love him. In my way.

EDITH: What do you mean, in your way?

RIKA: He looked after me. I appreciated that.

EDITH: Appreciated? What word is that to describe a relationship?

RIKA: He looked after me.

EDITH: Looked after is what you'd expect of a father.

RIKA: He wasn't Papa. He could never be Papa to me.

EDITH: Poor Paul. He never knew what he was up against. He never realised he could've lived a million years it would never have ..

RIKA: It's true.

EDITH: I always liked him. A bit of a nebbish, but, likeable. Kind. A good egg, they say, don't they?

RIKA: Nu

EDITH: But you loved him at the beginning. You obviously had sex with him. I mean after all there is Laura..

RIKA: Sex, Edith? Is that all you can think about?

EDITH: Why won't you talk about it?

RIKA: What's there to talk? It's the most boring, over-rated, uninteresting topic you can possibly think of.

EDITH: Oh, I don't know. Don't you ever get a bit, you know, if you're watching something on television, you get into the story, you feel for the characters. And then, the music, they start.. Don't you then, you know?

RIKA: I switch channels. That's what I do.

EDITH: When did you stop being interested…

RIKA: I was never interested.

EDITH: Oh yes you were.

RIKA: Stop, Edith. I don't want this conversation.

EDITH: You were. You were interested.

RIKA: Edith. I don't want to talk about it.

EDITH: I remember, something, years back…

What was it again? It was you, and, some… what happened again. It was, night. There'd been some problem or something. You remember, don't you Rika. Your long term memory's not supposed to go. You must remember.

RIKA: I don't remember.

EDITH: Of course you do. Something happened, with you. You and … who was it for goodness' sake!

RIKA: My God, Edith. You are the most extraordinary woman.

EDITH: Why? What have I done?

RIKA: You just forget whatever you want to. You're actually very lucky. My God it certainly makes life easy for you.

EDITH: I'm seventy five. I'm allowed to forget.

RIKA: Allowed? Who gives you permission to forget things like that, things that have completely, de, completely, de, determined my life.

That's what your actions have done. Determined my life. And you don't even remember it. You have the cheek to forget…

EDITH: What happened for God's sake?

RIKA: Forget it.

EDITH: Tell me Rika. I want to know.

RIKA: Oh, die in ignorance.

EDITH: Please tell me, Rika.

(Pause.)

RIKA: That poor child.

EDITH: Who?

RIKA: That poor, vulnerable… Who? Me that's who. Desperate for some of that warmth, that tenderness I'd left behind, that I'd, forgotten. That's all I wanted really. That's why I went there, just for some, kindness.

EDITH: Went where?

RIKA: I can even smell it. That musty, slightly seeweedy smell of his room. Dirty white really. No real colour on the walls. And the cup next to his bed, and in it, at the bottom mud, the stuff that's left after you drink Turkish coffee. And the curtains that don't quite meet, and, the narrow bed. The scratchy, khaki blanket. No sheets. Just one pillow. And a biscuit, half-eaten that he must've put down when I walked in the door. He'd been reading Hemingway's 'The Old Man and the Sea'. To teach himself English.

EDITH: My God.

RIKA: He wasn't interested. Not really. I started to cry. He comforted me.

EDITH: You'd run away.

RIKA: I'd come to my sister.

EDITH: And went instead to Natan.

RIKA: He said 'Come little one, tell me why you're crying.'
'I'm lonely,' I said. 'Let me help you forget,' he said.

(Pause.)

His kiss was so soft. I loved the touch of his mouth against
mine, his tongue gently feeling its way into my mouth.

EDITH: Come on, Rika. Do we really need this?

RIKA: He pushed me down, carefully onto that small bed. His
hands were rough on my breasts. But he didn't linger. He
pushed my skirt up, pulled my knickers down.

EDITH: Rika, Please.

RIKA: Pushed himself into me. I think I felt pain. I know I
could feel the warmth of the liquid as it slipped down my
legs. Red. Thick.

(Pause.)

But, that was it. That was all there was because, the next
moment, the very next moment, the door flew open, and
… You remember now, don't you Edith?

(EDITH says nothing.)

You stood there. Just stood there. He got up. Got dressed.
I still lay on the bed, my knickers not even off me, down
there somewhere, by my feet. I was covered in blood, in
semen.

EDITH: He got you a towel.

RIKA: It was so rough.

EDITH: He took a cigarette.

RIKA: And lit one for you.

EDITH: You didn't move.

RIKA: Eventually. I got up and left. Left the two of you
together, smoking your cigarettes.

(Pause.)

Why did you come and look for me at Natan's?

EDITH: I wasn't looking for you. I didn't even know you were there.

RIKA: So why did you go there?

EDITH: Why? Because, because..

(Long pause.)

Oh for God's sake, Rika. Everyone was sleeping with him!

(RIKA slaps EDITH hard across the cheek, is upset but also appalled at her own behaviour. She collapses into a chair, crying. EDITH is shocked by what has happened and by RIKA's tears. After a while, she approaches her, as if to comfort her.)

EDITH: Rika. *(She tries to touch her but Rika pulls away.)*

Rika! Mensch!

RIKA   Don't mensch me, you, you, mad sex maniac you.

EDITH: Oy, me a sex maniac! Honestly!

RIKA: You had Joseph! You couldn't just leave me one, the one... in my whole life...

(Pause.)

EDITH: Strictly speaking, I was there first.

RIKA: Oh my God.

EDITH: Yes. I should be cross with you.

RIKA: Oh shut up! Shut up, you lying, evil, uhh, uhh, witch! You witch you!

EDITH: But I'm not cross with you. I'm not. It was just those times.

RIKA: You're disgusting. And that sweet Joseph..

EDITH: It didn't last long with Natan!

RIKA: Oh, so when you finished with him, you just went off, found, someone else.

EDITH: It wasn't like that!

RIKA: What would Mutti say if she knew you turned out to be a nymphomaniac.

EDITH: That word she can remember!

RIKA: She'd be disgusted with you!

EDITH: Oh stop it, Rika. I'm sorry about you and Natan.

RIKA: There never was a me and Natan. Me and Natan lasted, ten minutes. Less with your interruption.

EDITH: I've never been very good with timing.

(Pause.)

You hit me!

RIKA: You deserved it. And anyway, all those times you hit me.

EDITH: We were children!

RIKA: You always got more in.

EDITH: Papa always came to your aid.

RIKA: Yes, you would've killed me, you meshuggeneh!

EDITH: I wouldn't have killed you!

RIKA: Anyway, I didn't hit you so hard. Hardly a mark.

EDITH: God save us from seventy one year olds who can hit like Ali whatsisname

RIKA: Ali whatsisname. What is his name?

EDITH: Who knows?

RIKA: Who knows!

(Long pause.)

RIKA: It was a long time before it finally penetrated into that stupid head of mine that I didn't mean a single thing to him.

EDITH: He was like that.

RIKA: It meant nothing. It was the same as finishing his biscuit. I wanted to be important to him.

EDITH: Why did we never speak about it?

RIKA: We carried on as always. And then, you simply forgot.

EDITH: Yes.

RIKA: Lucky you.

(Pause.)

I used to dream a dream, the same one for years.

EDITH: I didn't know that

RIKA: I'd wake up, sit up, and there you'd be in the corner of the room. My safe room at home with Paul in England. You'd be there. Looking at me, puffing on your cigarette. Putting your cigarette out on my carpet, my Axminster, grinding it in with your naked toes. Then I'd realise, I was still asleep.

The phone suddenly rings, startling both of them. EDITH answers it.

EDITH: Hullo. …. No, no don't come now.

She puts the phone down.

Blackout

SCENE 4

It is the next morning. EDITH is sitting in the chair, reading the paper and drinking coffee. RIKA walks in wearing her dressing gown, half awake.

RIKA: She hasn't phoned, huh?

EDITH: Not yet.

RIKA: If she doesn't phone, she might just turn up. You know, at the airport.

EDITH: She won't do that. She'll phone.

RIKA: Yah. I'm sure she will. I hope she's seen sense.

EDITH: It all depends on the definition of sense.

(Pause.)

RIKA: Sense is something that's very closely woven into our own selfish wishes.

EDITH: What?

RIKA: You always wanted a child.

EDITH: What's the connection? We're talking about sense and you come up with…. Anyway, I had lots of childrem in the kibbutz… I was close to so many.

RIKA: Edith. Don't. Lying is one thing. Pretending to yourself is something else completely. You always wanted a child. You never had one. Now you have the chance of having mine.

EDITH: Rika, if you honestly believe that..

RIKA: It's either that, or that you can't bear me to have something you can't have.

EDITH: Do you honestly think I want you to be unhappy.

RIKA: I think you want to be happier than me. Always. That your reference of happiness is whether it's greater than mine.

EDITH: Why must everything be in relation to you?

RIKA: Because you need to know that things are better for you than they are for me.

EDITH: Things always have been better for me. I am happier than you. I always have been. But, never at your expense. I swear to the God I don't believe in, I have never wanted you to be unhappy.

RIKA: Just less happy than you.

EDITH: I've never needed a barometer to check out my level of happiness. I was surrounded by friends, had a loving husband whot did whatever I wanted him to do..

RIKA: You bullied him too.

EDITH: …had a cause that I believed in passionately….

RIKA: Even though you were wrong about it…

EDITH: …lived with sunshine in my homeland.

RIKA: But didn't have a child.

EDITH: Lots of people don't have children.

RIKA: Lots of people don't want children.

EDITH: Exactly!

RIKA: But you did.

> *(Pause.)*

> And I had one. And if that wasn't bad enough, I had a grandchild. A beautiful grandchild who grew into a lovely, delightful eighteen year old. And it really is just a little bit too much for you.

EDITH: Of course I want Janine to stay here. Of course for me, but for her too. Why wouldn't I want it for her? She's living the life we lived, the pioneering life. In kibbutzim now life all so much easier, kushier. But where she is, that kibbutz there in the desert, it's still dangerous.

RIKA: My God, you said it wasn't dangerous!

EDITH: Not dangerous, just, less civilised. That's what I mean. She'll have the opportunity to really experience something life-enhancing. Compared to what you want to offer her. To sit around those horrible pubs they have all over the place on campuses, drinking, smoking, taking drugs.

RIKA: No not Janine.

EDITH: They all do it. She's at risk of doing it. But here, it's safer...

RIKA: Here? What's safer here? Suicide bombers, terrorism, even the Israeli soldiers have become brutal. It's not the same as your days. It's a different world, a different life.

EDITH: Life is more useful here. You live a cause.

RIKA: No. Not anymore.

EDITH: Yes. Still. We need people. We need young people who will have children

RIKA: To go into the armies and fight and kill.

EDITH: Defend. Allow us to carry on living here. In our homeland.

RIKA: I don't want my grandchild to be cannon fodder.

EDITH: It's not your choice.

RIKA: And it's not yours.

EDITH: So. We'll have to wait and see then.

RIKA: We will.

   Pause.

EDITH: You're wrong, you know.

RIKA: Of course. That's always been my role for you.

EDITH: Stop it already.

RIKA: So what am I wrong about this time?

The phone suddenly rings. They both grab it. RIKA gets it.

Hello? Oh, it's you. No not yet. Anyway, here she is. *(She hands it to EDITH.)* It's your boyfriend.

EDITH: Hello? Ahh, Natan. No we were just expecting a call from Janine, that's all. ... No, not then. I'll be tired, the airport and everything. ... Leave it a bit Natan. I'll speak to you. .... No, it's nothing. Just leave it. Bye.

She replaces the receiver. RIKA looks at her.

You were wrong about your happiness. I really want you to be happy. I hate the fact you're not.

The phone rings again. This time RIKA lets EDITH answer it.

Hello. Ah, it's you my sweetheart. How are you? .... Fine, good. ... Yes, we're fine.... We've been, reminiscing. Talking about the old days. It's been fun. Well, I've had fun! Sometimes your grandmother gets annoyed with me. I can't understand why. ... No, I'm only joking. Listen, she wants to speak to you. She's looking very anxious. Here she is.

She hands the phone to RIKA who goes into the bedroom. EDITH tries to listen at the door but can't hear. She paces the room worried until Rika returns.

EDITH: What's happened?

RIKA: She's coming home.

EDITH: Is she?

RIKA: But only for a few months.

EDITH: Only a few months?

RIKA: To make money.

EDITH: To make money?

RIKA: So she can travel.

EDITH: She's going travelling?

RIKA: To the East. Thailand, India, all that sort of thing.

EDITH: With Ari?

RIKA: No. With a girl. A girl friend she met at the kibbutz. Someone I hadn't heard of before.

EDITH: Oy vay.

RIKA: I know. Oy. Two girls alone in the whole of the East.

EDITH: India!

RIKA: India!

EDITH: But it's so...

RIKA: dangerous

EDITH: the monkeys

RIKA: the poverty

EDITH: life's so cheap

RIKA: she could be

EDITH: just

RIKA Killed.

EDITH: Stabbed

RIKA: Who knows?

EDITH: Who would help?

RIKA: She could get lost

EDITH: Could get mugged

RIKA: I read about someone just the other day, mugged, murdered, hung on a tree

EDITH: Oh my God!

RIKA: India!

EDITH: India!

RIKA: All those beggars

EDITH: All that filth

EDITH &RIKA: I don't like it.

RIKA: She's so young.

EDITH: Only eighteen.

RIKA & EDITH: Oy Edith! Oy Rika *(Said together.)*

(Long pause.)

EDITH: I'd rather she went to university.

RIKA: I'd rather she stayed here.

EDITH: We've both lost out.

RIKA: We have. Can we stop her.

EDITH: You know we can't.

RIKA: We could say…

EDITH: You were ill.

RIKA: Seriously ill. Suddenly.

EDITH: She'd expect me to look after you.

RIKA: Why should you look after me?

EDITH: I'm your sister, that's why. I should look after you.

RIKA: We can say, you're seriously ill.

EDITH: That's silly. She knows I'm as strong as an ox.

RIKA: You're seventy five. You're actually not so strong, you know.

EDITH: Like an ox!

RIKA: No, not like an ox. Like a goat. A skinny, sickly goat.

EDITH: I'm far more an ox than a goat.

RIKA: And me?

EDITH: A cat. A cat with nine lives.

RIKA: Hmm.

(Pause.)

We've got to let her go.

EDITH: There's nothing we can do.

RIKA: There's nothing we should do.

EDITH: It's her life.

RIKA: Her life to make her mistakes in it.

EDITH: Like we did.

RIKA: Yes. Like we did. Just like we did.

(Pause.)

Nu. I'd better get a move on, get going.

EDITH: You don't have to, Rika. You could come and live here. In the kibbutz?

RIKA: With you?

EDITH: Yes, with me.

RIKA: Do you think so?

EDITH: Why not?

RIKA: I could really, couldn't I?

EDITH: Of course.

RIKA: After all, we are sisters.

EDITH: We don't have anybody else.

RIKA: It could be nice

EDITH: Yes, it could be nice. We know how to laugh together.

RIKA: Of course we do. We know how to have fun

EDITH: Be together.

Pause

RIKA: We'd drive each other nuts.

EDITH: No we wouldn't.

RIKA: We'd end up crazy. Mad. We'd kill each other.

EDITH: Well, that's one way to go.

RIKA: There are quicker ways.

EDITH: You can stop me making a stupid move with that Natan.

RIKA: That fool.

EDITH: Yes, imagine at my age. Starting with him.

RIKA: Ridiculous.

EDITH: Yes.

RIKA: It'll be like giving in, if I move here with you.

EDITH: No, it won't.

RIKA: It'll be giving up my independence.

EDITH: At our age, independence is something we can do without.

RIKA: You'll bully me.

EDITH: I'll be as good as gold.

RIKA: You'll drive me mad with your, your sex, and your nonsense.

EDITH: You'll drive me mad first with your worrying.

RIKA: It is tempting.

EDITH: Go on, Rika. We're old. We've only got each other now. We're all we've got.

RIKA: You've got the world, Edith.

EDITH: I want you to have it too.

RIKA: Some people just fit it better. Visits are also good.

EDITH: Rika, you know what? Hidden from you, in the bottom most depth of my wardrobe, is a packet of biscuits, so good, that you, in your entire life, have never tasted anything like it. And I am going to get them out and give you one.

RIKA: One?

EDITH: One!

RIKA: Why would I want one?

EDITH: Alright already, have two!

BLACK

WWW.OBERONBOOKS.COM